Leonard Isaacs: Five Lives in One

Leonard Isaacs
1909 – 1997

SELECTED MEMOIRS

Leonard Isaacs

Five Lives in One

EDITED BY MARGARET ISAACS

Good Cheer Publishing ❖ *Hubbards, Nova Scotia*

**Canadian Cataloguing in
Publication Data**

Main entry under title:

Five Lives in One

Includes index.
ISBN 0-9681444-1-1

1. Isaacs, Leonard, 1909-1997
2. Pianists – Canada – Biography
I. Isaacs, Margaret, 1960-
II. Five Lives in One

ML417.I73A3 1998   786.2'092
C98-950138-8

© 1998 Good Cheer Publishing
RR2, Hubbards, Nova Scotia
B0J 1T0

Book design: Geoffrey Hayes
Typography: Savi Communications
Cover photograph: V. Tony Hauser

Printed in Canada by Premier Printing Ltd.

Contents

Editor's Note

*D*AD WROTE HIS MEMOIRS early in 1996. It was actually his third try at this project. A number of friends and family had been prodding him for a while, to put some of his experiences on paper; and from time to time he had dabbled at it. Several people had tried transcribing his chicken-scratch handwriting into typewritten pages, but these were only bits and pieces of his life stories. Finally, one day in February 1996, I think it was, he emerged from his room and said, "Well, I've written them. Now, who's going to read them?" And so, since he'd done his part of the bargain, I started in on mine!

Our work together continued from that day right up until about three weeks before he died. The last photo in this book was taken at about the same time as Mom faxed to me the last details I had requested from him. They were just as lucid and illuminating as everything else he wrote; no mental "tailing off" as his death drew near.

Dad was a very private person, though he was a very public professional, and he bent over backwards to respect the privacy of others too, so it was sometimes like pulling teeth to get him to refer to people by name in some situations, instead of in the oh-so-polite "third person". Still and all, these two years working back and forth with him on the details of his memoirs, have allowed me to know my father in a way that nothing else could. Except perhaps making music with him. When we would be rehearsing something, Brahms or Schumann, he'd get so exasperated if I wanted to talk it through. "Don't *talk* about it; just *do it*" he'd say; which is pretty much how he has lived his own life.

I have not changed his words, except occasionally when his sentences ran for half a page! Yes, he could do that. Any elaborations which I have contributed, he read and gave his approval to. Hopefully you won't notice a big change in style in these places... and no, I'm not going to tell you where they occur!

My deepest appreciation to Geoffrey Hayes for designing and putting the book together; to Good Cheer Publishing and Jacqui Good, for her knowledge, encouragement, professional guidance and proof-reading! Thanks also to Don Anderson for allowing us to use his headline "Five Lives in One" as part of the title for the book; to Victor Feldbrill for his eloquent words of introduction; and to the Globe and Mail and William Neville for allowing us to reprint his "Lives Lived" column from that newspaper. To my sister Naomi, many thanks for clarifying some information, and for providing me with pictures of herself, her Mom, and Mélisande! A huge thank you to my Mom, for taking care of so much of the "detail stuff" and faxing of things; and, like my sister Debbie, for her incredible patience with the pace of my work. I wish I could thank Dad too, for writing this. I think that's the one thing I forgot to say to him.

Enjoy!

Margaret Isaacs, Editor

Preface

As I sat reading this manuscript of my late colleague and friend Leonard Isaacs, I was struck immediately by the honesty and modesty of his words. His recollections cover a most significant period of music making not only in Canada, where he lived for thirty-five years, but also in the United Kingdom, where he was born and educated.

It was in England where he was working for the BBC that I first met Leonard, when I appeared as a guest conductor for the BBC Northern Orchestra in Manchester. Our friendship began instantly, and was further developed when he became the head of the new music department at the University of Manitoba. During the late sixties which were my last, somewhat turbulent, years as Music Director of the Winnipeg Symphony, his presence was a source of great strength and support. I shall always remember Leonard for that.

His unostentatious wealth of musical knowledge, his no-nonsense honesty and delightful sense of humour; all the qualities I found in him throughout our long friendship, are abundantly represented in Leonard's memoirs.

Victor Feldbrill, o.c.
Toronto, May 27, 1998

$\equiv$ I $\equiv$
Manchester
Family Background and School Years

$\mathcal{F}$OR SOMEONE WHO was going to spend his life almost totally immersed in music, I suppose it could be said that I had a most auspicious start. My father, Edward Isaacs, was a concert pianist (a pupil of Olga Neruda and Ferruccio Busoni); his forbears had come to Manchester, England, at some unknown date in the early 1800s, possibly from Odessa. I never have known for certain, and nor did my father. My mother, Amy Jordan, played the violin. Her father, Albert Jordan, had come from Hamburg; one of those many German merchants who had settled in Manchester and helped sustain its musical life. For the Jordan family, who lived outside Manchester, in Bowdon, Cheshire, music was an integral part of life.

Grandmother Emma Jordan died when my mother was still a baby, so the eldest daughter, Daisy, brought up my mother. There was 17 years between them, "Auntie D" having been born in 1866, and my mother in 1883. Daisy played violin, viola, and trumpet. The last-named was a source of breath-taking delight to me; it looked both inviting and exciting in its velvet-lined case. Occasionally I was allowed to try and blow it, but I rarely got a sound out of it! Auntie Daisy was a tremendous influence in my young life.

Next to her in age was Nelly, the only Jordan who played the piano. She married the German cellist Carl Fuchs[1] who had come to England in 1887 to see Sir Charles Hallé, with an introductory letter from Clara Schumann. He became Hallé's principal cellist and also a member of the

Brodsky String Quartet[2].

Then there was Uncle Alf Jordan, a radiologist, who lived in London and played viola. His wife Christine was a splendid violinist. Uncle Francis who lived in Hale, near Manchester, and was a businessman, played the cello. Aunt Rose, born in 1875, was the next in age and she, like Alf, was a doctor, though while her father Albert was alive, she was not allowed to study medicine. The closest he would let her get was to study Botany. Accordingly, when he died in 1899, she immediately entered Medicine, and became one of the first woman doctors in England. She lived in London, and was Tuberculosis Officer for the district of Lewisham. She was the only Jordan who played no instrument.

My mother Amy was the youngest of the family. Her violin teacher was Rawdon Briggs, the second violin of the Brodsky Quartet and principal second violin in the Hallé Orchestra. She and my father had met as students at the Royal Manchester College of Music. My family's friends and acquaintances too, were mostly musicians; including the Catteralls[3] and the Merricks[4]; and the 14 year old Elie Spivak who came from Russia to study with Brodsky, and whom I met again later in Toronto.

With all these musicians in and around the family, it is really small wonder that my earliest recollections are of tunes rather than of people or places. It seems as though the Tchaikovsky *Piano Concerto No. 1* and the finale of the Beethoven *Violin Concerto* had been born into me; they are indeed the very first things in life that I can remember! Dad had been working at the Tchaikovsky when I was born, and my mother used to "get me accustomed to the violin" (as she said) by playing me the opening of the finale of the Beethoven opus 61. I simply never remember a time when I did not hear music.

From about the age of 6, I was taken to chamber music concerts; either string quartets or quintets, or else including a piano and strings work, with the pianist either my father or another of the good Manchester pianists, Max Mayer or Isidor Cohn. Or it might be R.J. Forbes, who succeeded Adolf Brodsky as Principal of the Royal Manchester College of Music; or, a little later, that excellent pianist and subsequently BBC accompanist, John Wills. And so I found, a while later, that I already knew works which I had imagined I was going to be hearing for the first time. For instance, in 1925 I heard the Lener Quartet[5] play all seventeen Beethoven String Quartets: I discovered that, tune after tune, they were already seemingly innately familiar to me! And all because of those concerts so early in my life!

I played on the piano as soon as I was able, and no one ever tried to discourage me; though I can still remember what trouble learning the bass clef gave me! However, as soon as I was ready for lessons, I worked at the things my father produced for me; Aloys Schmidt exercises, easier Czerny and "technique". And of course plenty of real music; Bach teaching-pieces and a few *Two-Part Inventions*; Mozart and Haydn, a little Beethoven, a few Chopin *Preludes*, Grieg *Lyric Pieces* (and the *Wedding Procession*, which was thrilling); and some Handel and Scarlatti. A good Classical background. By the time I was eleven I had a reasonable technique, and was prepared to make music with other people.

One never-to-be-forgotten summer (1920; I was now eleven and a half), the whole Jordan family, Manchester and London contingents, joined for a holiday in North Wales, at a place called Fairbourne, just south of Barmouth in Merionethshire. The whole family, numbering 18 or 19 grown-ups and children (I am not sure if Aunt Rose was with us) took two adjacent houses, and every night there was chamber music: quartets by Haydn, Mozart, Beethoven, Schubert, Brahms, Smetana, and Debussy; quintets by Mozart and Brahms, and sextets too. We could even raise eight players for the Mendelssohn and Glière octets, though my cousin Marjorie Jordan, the fourth violin, was only 10!

My sister Ruth was with us too, but being still only seven, she was not yet ready to join in the music-making. Later in life she became a quite good pianist and violinist. I too had tried the violin (to please my mother) and, that being highly unsuccessful, I tried the cello too. But after a few lessons with Uncle Carl, he said to me "Leonard, you'd better stick to the piano!" One of the two houses in which we spent that summer boasted a very old piano, of the kind the Jordans called a P.S.O. (piano-shaped object). My father wouldn't even try it, but I was anxious to. I was permitted to play Rheinberger and Beethoven *Piano Quartets* with the family. I heard so much music that summer! I think it was that which made chamber music one of my chief joys for ever thereafter.

Apart from the summers, I was of course, at school in Manchester. I thoroughly enjoyed the kindergarten I attended, about five minutes' walk from home. And as no one thought that one went to school other than to learn, learn I did. This included some French, so that by age eight I had a reasonable vocabulary, though no conversational fluency. German I had been able to speak quite fluently up to the age of five (the Fuchses spoke German at home as a matter of course), but after 1914 one didn't speak German out and about anymore, and so I forgot it and had to relearn it later on. I could read anything in English, and write too. At the age of eight I wrote a highly unscientific (not to say inaccurate!) survey of some extinct animals. My uncle David Isaacs was secretary to Professor Ray Lankester at the Manchester School of Technology, and he solemnly told me he had shown the ms to the Professor, who had "commended its author's industry but questioned some of his facts"... I was a bit damped by this!

Also at the age of eight, I changed schools; in my estimation for the worse, since I had loved kindergarten and found my new school, South Manchester Preparatory Grammar School rather forbidding; and all boys. But I soon got used to the peculiar behaviour of one or two of the teachers, and got used, too, to being called by my surname. Additionally, I discovered that I could, after all, transfer my affection from Miss Adeline at kindergarten to my new form-mistress, Miss McEwen. The War had made the advent of female teachers into boys' schools unavoidable, since so many male teachers were in the Armed Forces.

Indeed, these Armed Forces were everywhere in evidence during my younger childhood. I can remember the day war was declared; August 4th, 1914. We were in a train on our way to a Welsh summer holiday (in Llanfairfechan or Aberdovey), and my father opened the newspaper and exclaimed "They've started the war!" I still remember, too, the smoke of the railway engine smelling like egg sandwiches! (There are people who think the reverse; that egg sandwiches smell like engine smoke, all sulphurous!) It was not long after this that one could meet men in uniform everywhere; a little later too, the wounded men in hospital-blue. My nurse Alice went out with one of them, a charming and handsome man called Jack Gledhill; I don't know if they subsequently got married. They would take me for walks in Birch Park (with my sister Ruth in a pram) and we'd study the gravestones in the churchyard, and, much more

exciting; see and listen to the Police Brass Band which played in the covered bandstand many an afternoon. I found the brass instruments most
enthralling, as I did Auntie Daisy's trumpet.

The "band-in-the-park" had a delicious sequel. At that age (I was
maybe 6 or 7) my father invented the most wonderful and comical stories to tell me, largely concerning a diminutive character called Mr.
Merlin. On one occasion Mr. Merlin, in flight from some danger,
jumped into the bell of a big tuba, and was subsequently blown out of
it by a large fat policeman. This caused gales of laughter; of course I
knew what a tuba was, and for many years afterwards I could recall the
imagined sight of the wee man being ejected from a tuba's wide bell, and
the laughter would be renewed. I never lost my delight in the brass
instruments, and eventually, at age 16, I started to learn the french horn.

These war years were also somewhat clouded by the presence, very
near to our house, of an anti-aircraft gun. I was scared of it, and of the
regular nightly display of searchlights. I had nightmares about all this. In
one of these the "aeroplane thunder-clouds" were coming; I could hear
the drone and was horribly frightened. I had been left out of doors to
await some great explosion which was expected, in the company of two
girls from my kindergarten, Peggy and Joan Dearden, both covered in
walnut icing! My parents had disappeared, and then the explosion happened. Good thing it was only a dream! But so vivid that I remember it
to this day.

Oddly enough, the names of my companions in kindergarten are still
with me; Claud and Lewis Frith, Esmé and Basil Gossage, Olive Worsley,
Edna Parrott, Freddie White. They all had birthday parties, at which one
played the most shame-making kissing games. I absolutely hated these,
though I certainly did like the food, especially the trifles, with cream and
almonds on top! And very clearly can I still see those two excellent
women who ran the school in their own house; Miss Thorpe and her
younger sister Miss Adeline. I owe them a very great deal; for three years
they opened our minds to much of the world, and they kept bigotry and
cruelty from us. We were all happy.

This happiness could not continue undimmed in a boys' school, and
it didn't. The teaching was more formalized and the pupil-teacher relationship was depersonalized. Humour among the staff was typified by a

master who used to call an Armenian boy named Fonduklian by the mocking "Herr von Duklian", causing him acute embarrassment, and the rest of us rather shame-faced amusement. There was another boy whose parents were naturalized Germans, and nobody would spend play-time with him. Privately, outside school hours, one could fraternize, and I did. His father kept the best delicatessen store in Manchester.

The day of the Armistice, November 11th, 1918, was made a half-holiday, and we all trooped home at mid-day.

My father was never "called up" on account of his poor eyesight, but he spent much time organizing and playing at concerts in hospitals. When I would get home from school each day, Dad would be practising or teaching. His own repertoire, before he lost his sight in 1923, was the big Chopin-Liszt one. I knew well from hearing them, all the Chopin *Ballades*, the *B flat minor and E major Scherzos*, the *B minor Sonata* (oddly enough, not the *Funeral March Sonata*), the *Concert-Allegro*, the *Bolero*; and many *Waltzes, Nocturnes*, and a couple of *Polonaises*. I cannot remember Dad ever playing any *Mazurkas* or *Preludes*, but some of the *Etudes* were favourites, particularly the "double-thirds" one. Of Liszt there was also plenty. I used often to sit under the piano, reading a book, while over my head the *C sharp minor Hungarian Rhapsody* or one of the *Paganini Etudes* would thunder away. I remember one particular book whose excitement was greatly heightened by the music of Liszt. It was called *The Desert Ship* and was about "Red Indians"; battles and torture and a beautiful Indian girl named "Allura". (And of course, a happy ending).

In the last year of his sightedness Dad prepared the Liszt *Sonata*, and I got to know every note of it; though I never have dared to try and play it! It was the last big work that Dad learned and played in recital. In December of 1923 a slip on the ice and a bad fall resulted in detachment of the retina of his only good eye. In those days, that was rarely curable. Dad ended up quite blind and was restricted to more manageable repertoire. He made a huge and sustained effort to re-learn the keyboard without sight. By degrees he triumphed over his disability, and much of his previous range of music became once more available. But not the Liszt *Sonata*!

From the days before he fell I remember also lots of Bach and

Beethoven, and some Debussy (notably *Pour le Piano*), a little Brahms; some Mozart and Haydn, and, along with Chopin and Liszt, one of his great favourites was the Mendelssohn *Prelude and Fugue in E minor*. He also played Liszt and Busoni transcriptions, which are, a bit stupidly, frowned upon nowadays. And there was a grand set of *Variations* by Alexandre Glazunov, which I loved (and even orchestrated!). I was therefore thrilled a few years later in Paris, when I was asked by a Russian girl cellist at the École Normale, to accompany her when she went to play to Glazunov. He was by then a rather heavy and slow-moving elderly man of 65, but in Anna Drittel's company I gazed awe-struck and reverently at this living legend; hadn't he known Balakirev (whose *Rêverie in F* my father played)? And wasn't he a pupil of Rimsky-Korsakov, whose *Scheherazade* I knew and loved?

But I must return to boyhood!

Altogether the four years I spent at South Manchester Preparatory Grammar School were not too bad, and at the age of 12 I finished there and went downtown to the real Manchester Grammar School. My father and uncles and male cousins had attended there too. It was a huge school: in my day about 1300 boys. It had a fine academic reputation. The school had been founded in 1515, during King Henry VIII's reign, by Hugh Oldham, Bishop of Exeter; so I was entering in the four hundred and fourth year of its existence!

The High Master in my time was a man of tremendous character, integrity and energy; John Lewis Paton[6]. When he retired from the MGS colossus in 1924, he went out to Newfoundland to head the new Memorial College there. Paton had a way of bringing distinguished and famous people with him into School Assembly in the morning, and having them speak to us. Among others I remember Lord Hewart of Bury, the then Lord Chief Justice and an Old Boy of the School, who was so moved that he was unable to speak; and the great Dr. Nansen, the super-famous explorer and inventor of the Nansen passport for stateless people, and the hero of the Russian Famine in 1921.

The Assembly was, in fact, School Prayers for all but the Orthodox Jewish boys and the Moslems; and the school organist was a boy named William Minay, a fine player indeed. (He went on to become a professional organist, and worked mostly in Scotland. He died in 1994.) It was here I first heard Parry's *Jerusalem*: Minay's introductory bars were magnificent! I have never again heard it played with such dignity and éclat. I was moved to literal tears, all twelve years of me!

Most unfashionably I enjoyed my three years at Manchester Grammar School (it was always known simply by its initials: MGS). Life opened up; the work got done; I joined the Boy Scouts (a most admirable substitute for "games") and had a very exciting, valuable and companionable time in Troop III. My cousin Edgar Fuchs (5 years older than I) was still at school, a Rover and later an Assistant Scoutmaster in the same Troop. So was his close friend Philip Lewis who was an excellent pianist and clarinetist, and a wonderful conjurer. I formed a piano duet team with Philip. I'd already discovered duets with a boy from South Manchester School who lived very near us; Frank McConnell. Frank and I would meet every so often to read through what duet music we could find. His mother was a piano teacher and there was quite a lot of music to be found! I remember with what delight we "discovered" the Brahms *Hungarian Dances*: the one in D flat got played 14 times through, non-stop!

But with Philip Lewis it was the Beethoven *Symphonies*. We soon co-opted a few string players and played #2, #4, and #6, and also I think #8 with piano à quatre mains, 2 or 3 violins, viola and cello. This group continued to exist after I'd moved to London, and I would come home for the holidays to find that we could arrange a Beethoven *Septet* or Schubert *Octet* (I was playing french horn as well, by then). Finally the group (known as the "Double-Fisters"; two fists at one piano) swelled into an orchestra which assembled a few times a year, the brass section filled out by members of the famous Fodens Works Band. The North of England was the home of many fine Brass Bands, such as the Black Dyke Mills Band, and the Besses o'th'Barn Band; splendid, flexible musical instruments, filled with highly skilled and enthusiastic individual players. Fodens was one of the best, and I fancy Cousin Edgar, who now worked for Imperial Chemical Industries, was the contact which produced some fine trumpet and trombone players. A couple of times I had the thrill of conducting this orchestra. What a transformation from the original piano duets! Half of musical Manchester became involved in the Double-Fisters before they finally finished, whenever that was.

I matriculated in 1923, in Classics (Latin, Greek, French, English, History and Maths) and then moved into a sort of pre-sixth form where one was groomed for the further three-year preparation for University. As a matter of interest and a gauge of the teaching we were afforded, out of a class of 23 boys, all but one matriculated, and the majority (of which I was one) got "distinction" (65% or more) in Latin and Greek, without being able to help it. I think that the three men I had as Form Masters during my time at MGS were models of what a good teacher can be. Each of them, Messrs. Warman, Dakers and Johnstone, was a civilized and cultivated person, with an interest in what he taught (I remember Mr. Johnstone telling us he read Horace in the evening for sheer pleasure: a level which few of us ever attained, I guess!). All three men were human beings, and as far as their duty permitted, they exuded friendliness and warmth. And we were indeed taught how to use our minds, regardless of the subject we were using them on.

I became deeply involved in the School's musical activities (all, by the way, extra-curricular); orchestra, lunch-hour recitals, study-circle, end of term concert performances of choral works, and so on. I began to feel that I couldn't take many more years of Greek and Latin. My new form-master, Mr. Johnstone, lent me a book entitled "Careers for Boys" which I read from cover to cover without finding any career which looked at all as if it would suit me, or I it. And at that point the amazing thought occurred to me, "well, my father is a musician, and my uncle Carl; I'd better be one too." And so it was.

I finished school at the end of July 1924, aged fifteen and a half, and took away with me great affection for some of the masters with whom I'd been living for the past while. Jack Rivers, the Scoutmaster, thin and dark and deeply serious; Heathcote, one of the men who kept music going at MGS; and Chevalier, (known as "Shandy"), the mathematician, whose sixth form would stay in school with him until 6 p.m. out of sheer fascination with him and his teaching. Shandy also played clarinet. I do not think he survived his efforts in Saint-Saëns's *Carnival of the Animals*, in which his instrument is the cuckoo. Shandy played it correctly, but his chronic catarrh didn't help in playing a wind instrument. He would snort in between the "cuck" and the "oo", which reduced the rest of the orchestra to hysterics! He was most horribly embarrassed, poor fellow. But he was a basically lovable man, and he was afraid of the music of J.S. Bach. One of my school-mates, C.J. Lockett and I tried to dispel this fear one afternoon by playing him as much Bach as we could; piano, violin and organ, between us. The payoff was typical of Shandy; the first time I was home from London I went back to school to see people there, and I paid a visit to Mr. Chevalier in his classroom. He looked up from his desk, and without saying "Good afternoon" or any other form of greeting, said "I wasted six shillings because of you." "Oh! How?" said I. "I bought Bach's *48 Preludes and Fugues:* can't play any of 'em!"

And then there was Mr. Lob. Red-haired, of medium height, wiry, Jewish, a man of enormous energy, enthusiasm and charm, Harry Lob taught mathematics; coached and organized the under-14 cricket teams; played chess, and a rather poor cello with unquenchable zeal. He used sometimes to take a group of boys to a Hallé Orchestra concert; he paid for us, and the evening would begin with supper (baked beans on toast or a poached egg) at Wynn's Café near the School. It was on one of Mr. Lob's evenings that I heard my first-ever Beethoven 5, and was greatly moved. Lob was the only member of the MGS academic staff to lose his life while on duty as an air-raid warden. He was blown to bits by a bomb, in Withington, quite near the White Lion Pub. He must have been mourned by thousands of men who went through his hands, and who, like me, had grown to love this curiously shy yet gregarious bachelor.

Each summer Mr. Lob would lead a trek through some part of Europe; boys, masters, and Old Mancunians (that is to say, "old boys" of the School). These treks became famous, or notorious, according to how you regarded them. They were always pretty strenuous. And my finale at MGS was to go on one of Lob's Treks in the summer of 1924, to Spain. There were close on 50 boys and 10 or a dozen adults. For camping each of our tents would hold four boys and one adult.

First of all there was Paris; we spent a day or two there on our way both to and from Spain. We wandered around the city, entranced: the Champs Elysées, the Jardin des Tuileries, the Madeleine, Notre Dame, the Louvre, the Invalides, the Eiffel Tower (and the old Trocadero was still there); and of course the Métro! It was easy finding one's way around, and my French proved adequate for guiding my companions, who seemed to know none! I little thought that in a few years' time I should be a student actually living in Paris.

The long train journey south from France was crowded and dirty, but on this first time away from England I was prepared to take what came, philosophically. The impressions we carried away from our trip to this northwest corner of Spain were varied. Beautiful scenery along the north coast; dry, parched interior; and a very hot and dusty Burgos. Some of the boys went to a bullfight, and wished they hadn't. In one little town we played a football match against the locals, resulting in a politically correct "draw". We saw the caves with prehistoric paintings; Altamira and Puente Viesgo; we visited the tiny town of Santillana, with its 10th century church with big, barred foot scrapers in front of the doors to keep the cows out!

We stayed in the commercial and industrial port of Bilbao, and upon leaving it in a westerly direction, marvelled at the strange formations of iron haematite. Further along the coast, in Santander, we met some Spanish Boy Scouts; and through camping on sandy ground we discovered that although mosquitoes may dislike Citronella oil, ants just *love* it: our tent was infested! Another olfactory camping disaster involved pitching tents near a field which had been manured with horrid smelly little fish! But we learned a few words of Spanish, and provided much amusement for the Basque children wherever we went. In our hiking rig-out we must have seemed pretty outlandish to them.

The crowning experience was the majesty of the Pyrenees, which we gradually approached on foot from Jaca, and then climbed, over the 7000 foot pass to Gavarnie. The violent contrast between the squalor of the last few Spanish villages on our route and the neat cleanliness of Gavarnie was startling, to say the least. But Gavarnie had to be kept attractive for the many travellers from Lourdes and elsewhere. They came to see the Cirque de Gavarnie with its high waterfall, which multiplied into a dozen when there was rain; as there definitely was for our visit!

I suppose the distance we actually walked added up to some 150 miles, plus the climb over the Pyrenees. It was very strenuous, and five weeks duration in all; but it was an experience which I wouldn't have missed for all the world! Though my subsequent visits to Europe were made without camping equipment, this excursion did something to prepare me for the future escapade with Maurice Hardy and Mélisande.

At any rate, I got back to London completely exhausted, and rested a few days in the home of my doctor-aunt Rose and her companion Rose Stern. Then, back to Manchester, to start on a heavy course of preparation towards winning a scholarship to one of the musical institutions in London. I would have to leave my home-town: my father had said "There's not room for the two of us here in Manchester", and *he* wasn't going to move anywhere!

Whatever impression I may have given up to now of my life as a boy, I must make it plain that there was more in it than just schoolwork and music. I certainly lived a full life; there was always time for hobbies and relaxation. In those days, of course, there was neither TV nor radio to clog the wheels of personal activity, and I became deeply interested and involved, at different times, in Palaeontology, Astronomy, Physiology, Philately, and Meccano! I had a fascinating box of playroom chemicals, with which I made awful stinks and drawing-room fireworks. I read everything I could lay my hands on (fiction and non-fiction alike) and was constantly and continuously employed.

I don't remember how much I practised the piano before 1925, but it must have been fairly regular, for my father sent me for lessons to one of his best local pupils, one Dorothy Crewe. I stayed with her until it was time to prepare for going to London, when Dad took over the instruction.

If my Dad was the great musical influence in my young life, there were two others whose influence was even wider: my Aunt Daisy and Uncle David. Those two supplied the impetus, nourishment and affection which I missed at home. My parents were kind to Ruth and me, and always generally supportive, but we did not receive much genuine overt affection, which they were equally unable to show to each other any longer. So my Aunt Daisy and my Uncle David became very special people for me.

Daisy never married; but she was anything but the typical "maiden aunt". There may have been some romance in her earlier life, but having had to assume responsibility for a large family upon her father's death in 1899, most other things were suppressed. She was short of stature, with short curly hair, long before it became de rigueur for women to wear it thus. She was eager and precise in speech, and unfailingly kind, loving and interesting. Her face was enormously alive, and I credited her with virtual omniscience! We used to say of her that "if Auntie Daisy didn't know something, she'd invent it, and her invention would be likely to be right"! We all idolized her! As a very small boy, I used to visit her in Hale, some 8 miles southwest of Manchester (the places named Altrincham, Hale, and Bowdon were continuous and indistinguishable). On our walks she would tell me the most wonderful and vivid tales; Greek and Norse mythology, Grimm fairy tales, and, most exciting of all, a tale of her own invention about how the local pub, the "Bleeding Wolf" came by its name, in times long gone by. It wasn't until many years later that I discovered that that pub was referred to locally as, naturally, the "Bloody Fox", which rather spoiled the story.

Daisy's company never palled, and for quite a long period I went to her for German lessons. She played viola or trumpet, as required, in an amateur orchestra conducted by Archie Camden[7], the principal bassoon of the Hallé Orchestra. I was sometimes taken to a rehearsal: there I heard Sibelius' *Valse Triste* for the first time, and there, too, Mr. Camden tried out a *Polonaise* which I had composed and orchestrated. That was indeed a thrill, and the result not too bad, considering that I was as yet a pretty inexperienced orchestrator.

Uncle David, my father's elder brother, was a totally different experience. He had never grown to a man's full physical stature. Some glandular defect or illness had caused him to remain as he had been at the age of 13; so he was little, treble-voiced, and not strong. But, as a child will, I accepted that "this is Uncle David" and I enjoyed his company unreservedly. He provided the intellectual ingredient in my developing life, where Auntie Daisy supplied the emotional and imaginative ones. As one might expect, Uncle David was an embittered person, but I was not then aware of this fact. (Rabbi Harold Kushner's deeply impressive book *When Bad Things Happen to Good People* was still 60 years in the future). David talked Religion, or Atheism, to me, and Socialism, Evolution, and Psychoanalysis (then very new); all, I suppose, unsuitable for a boy of my age. But I found his information enthralling, and his company enlivening and satisfying. He is almost solely respon-

sible for how I think, still! David lived on the north side of Manchester
with his mother (my Granny) and his sister Stella, who married when I
was nine or ten. Her marriage to Alec Jacobs was happy and successful;
of her two sons, my cousins, the elder, Arthur Jacobs, became a musician,
critic and editor, whose *Penguin Dictionary of Music* is still a valuable
book. Though Granny and Aunt Stella both lived to well over 80, Uncle
David didn't even reach 50. And no one else on my father's side of the
family ever made so great an impression on me.

I do not remember my sister Ruth being so much enamoured with
family as I was. Maybe I do her an injustice, but I cannot ask her, for she
died some years ago. At any rate, both of us were made welcome by
Auntie D. in Hale and by the Fuchs family too. In 1919 Uncle Carl
returned from Germany where he had been caught by the outbreak of
war, and he and his family moved into a house very near us in South
Manchester. For the 5 years before that the two sisters, Daisy and Nelly
(Carl's wife) had joined forces, and together with the two Fuchs boys,
my cousins Arnold and Edgar, had all shared the house in Hale.

This house had originally belonged to the Uncles George and Franz
Loewenthal, half-brothers of my grandmother Emma Jordan. George
became a naturalized Englishman, smoked cigars, and didn't care much
about music; he preferred his garden. He died before the war was over,
though the legacy of his cigars lingered on in the house long after he
had gone. Uncle Franz never bothered about citizenship, so he was
interned in Handforth; dear, harmless, inoffensive man that he was; and
after the War was shipped back to Germany. There he joined up with
Uncle Carl's elder sister, Wally, and kept a joint establishment in
Jugenheim an der Bergstrasse, where I met them in 1926 and again
in 1930.

My visits to the Fuchs house in Hale ("Inglenook", Ashley Road)
were frequent in the last couple of years of the War. Arnold and Edgar
were stimulating companions, and rather awe-inspiring elder brother
types. I still associate pillow fights with them, and learning the Morse
Code; and watching them use a heliograph in the garden, to a spot quite
a distance away. And they had *Harmsworth's Encyclopedia*, from which I
learned an enormous amount about monorail cars, astronomical
distances, lunar landscapes, and much general information; animal,

vegetable, and mineral!

About this time too, I must have begun to make acquaintance, at home in Manchester, with the music of the Savoy Operas. A year or two later, my mother was playing in the orchestra for the annual Gilbert and Sullivan season at the Opera House in Quay Street, and I began my introduction to these delicious pieces of theatre. Also the glittering stars of the D'Oyly Carte Company of those days; Sir Henry Lytton, Bertha Lewis, Leo Sheffield, Darrell Fancourt, Derek Oldham, Helen Gilliland; and the musical director Harry Norris (whom I met again in Montreal in 1931).

One annual Jordan family ceremony deserves mention: it took place at Auntie Daisy's in Hale until the Fuchses had a house of their own, then it was taken over by them. This was Christmas, celebrated in German style, with as many of the Jordan family together as possible. It never seemed to bother my father, who had been brought up in close association with the Synagogue, that he should be taking part in so foreign a ritual. There was in fact, nothing religious about the Christmas festivities of the Jordans and Fuchses. There might be as many as 18 or 19 people at the dinner table. The main course was roast goose; for weeks afterwards there'd be goose-dripping (Gänseschmalz) for breakfast! Auntie Nelly would have made an enormous Heringsalat, which she'd started days ahead, and Christmas Plum Pudding. The grown-ups all drank hock, brought over in a barrel from Germany by Uncle Carl, and decanted at home. The children were considered too young for such frivolity, but I rather minded being thus belittled. One year I crept back into the dining-room and drained the dregs of every glass; with, I may say, no ill effects. The "Bescherung" (handing out of presents) happened after a suitable interval from dinner, in a different room, and the excitement was always tremendous! Every person present, child and grown-up alike, had a special place, and there was a huge Christmas tree with real lighted candles. In those days, no one seemed to think of the possibility of a fire. There were decorations too, including a chocolate initial for each member of the gathering. In such circumstances it was inevitable, and also very happy, that the gang of cousins who met for these occasions would grow up feeling closer to one another than is often the case with first cousins. For a short period we also had the company of our

South American cousin Albert, the eldest son of the one Jordan who had emigrated and lived in Buenos Aires[8]. Albert came to England to finish his studies in engineering. I still regret not having been able to get to know the whole of that branch of the family.

The Fuchses also had a cottage in the hills on the borders of Cheshire and Derbyshire; "Foxhome", Whaley Bridge. A good 45 minutes' walk from the railway station, uphill all the way; but worth the exertion once you got there. The little house was perched on a hillside, in lovely hilly and wooded country. I visited there often. There was no electricity, just oil lamps; only outdoor sanitation, and a rill ran through a little ravine in the garden. Arnold and Edgar had built a dam, which produced a small pond, and there were flowers everywhere. I found it idyllic, especially in springtime. I would lie on the hillside, just by the house, and stay utterly silent and still, listening to the larks and the peewits overhead, and to the distant sound of barking dogs coming up from Kettleshulme in the valley far below. This quiet solitude was wonderful to me then, as is the memory of it now.

In the cottage there were books (though no piano) and it was here that I met Edward Whymper and his book *Scrambles Among the Alps*. Whymper was the first man to reach the top of the Matterhorn, in the mid-19th century, and the story of the climb made exciting reading. I loved the names of those Swiss mountains; Weisshorn, Finsteraarhorn, Jungfrau, Eiger, Mönch, Aletschhorn; as I also loved the North Welsh ones; Carnedd Llewellyn, Carnedd Davydd, Tal-y-Fan, Cader Idris, Carreg Fawr; they sounded wild, evocative.... I read Mr. Whymper over and over again, though I never had the stamina to become a mountaineer.

I was never any good at sports; I couldn't run fast, and football and lacrosse seemed rough and pointless to me. Cricket was tolerable, especially if I was deep in the outfield and could day-dream! But I was afraid of the terribly hard ball, and my eyes were not able to follow it up the pitch, so I usually missed both hitting and catching it! At MGS the Scouts made a very satisfactory alternative to organized games, and were, moreover, productive.

At home I had books, a microscope, a small hand telescope, an atlas, a planisphere, several stamp albums, and a set #5 Meccano, mentioned earlier. There could hardly be a dull moment, and there rarely was. When I was 9, Aunt Rose invited me for a week or so to her home in London, and I then made my first train journey alone, all of four hours! The visit was a huge success, from my point of view, anyway: I was introduced to Westminster Abbey, St. Paul's, the British Museum, the Natural History Museum, and the London Tube. The British Museum interested me the most; its variety was almost incredible. One day I found my way there on my own, and returned in triumph, with a book on colloquial Japanese. Auntie Rosie laughed, and well she might! I never used the book; I was stymied already in the first chapter.

Looking back on these various happenings from more than 75 years ago, I realize how rich my boyhood was, and how wide-ranging my interests. Apart from "games", life was rewarding and exciting; my good fortune was immense. There were horrors, it is true, but they were to be avoided or ignored if at all possible. I found a book in Uncle Alf's library which contained photographs of people with various forms of goitre, including one which haunted me for years, of a "coprophagous cretin". It was better not to think of such things. I knew something of the bestiality of war, as well as its heroism, but those years made me a life-long pacifist. Generally, the world was a completely fascinating place; and behind it all there was Music, which I now realize was always the most expressive language for me.

Such was my life until the age of fifteen and a half, when I started to prepare in earnest for the Associated Board Grade 8 Examination which I was to take in just under a year's time.

The next ten months were spent in practising towards that Associated Board exam, through which, if I did well enough, I might win a scholarship to either the Royal College or the Royal Academy of Music in London. My piano teacher for that year was my father: I don't suppose I've ever worked harder or had more terrifying lessons! In the end, it did pay off, though.

We rented time and practise space from some friends, name of Crampton, who owned a decent upright piano. Their elder daughter Kit was a violin student under Dr. Brodsky, and she used to regale me with tales about the fearful temper tantrums he would throw during lessons. Once he even bit right through the stem of his pipe in his rage! From my point of view now, some seventy-odd years later, that sort of behaviour seems very dated, and it was in any case ineffectual; Kit played neither better nor worse for it.

I could, and did, play accompaniments for her; thus I learned the Beethoven, Mendelssohn, and Bruch *Violin Concertos*, plus Bach and Mozart too. And I also learned a large part of the Gilbert and Sullivan operas, for Kit and her sister Helen were enthusiasts. We would get the libretti and scores from the Public Library, and spend hours playing and singing, to our enormous pleasure. I worked (or played) every day in that house.

I also took harmony lessons from Dr. Willcocks, the organist of Manchester Cathedral. I enjoyed them, for he was a kindly man with a clear mind and a constructive interest in what he taught. The supposedly dry subject held no terrors for me; I found it absorbing. Besides piano and theory, I attended as many rehearsals of the Hallé Orchestra as I had time for. The conductor, Hamilton Harty, had given my father permission for this, and I was mesmerized. Under Harty's baton I made my acquaintance with a very wide range of orchestral music. Most of the Very Greats, like Beethoven 5 and 9, the Brahms *Requiem*, Bach's *B minor Mass*, *Messiah*, the Schubert *C major*, Berlioz' *Fantastique*; I heard for the first time in my life, at his hands. I remember Harty as a very musical and vital man with a flair for the dramatic (his Irish blood, perhaps?). Before becoming a conductor he had been a first-class piano-accompanist. Harty's sympathies were as much with singers as with instrumentalists. It was as a solo pianist that he took part in the first performance of Constant Lambert's *Rio Grande* in 1929. His wife was Miss (later Dame) Agnes Nicholls, one of England's finest oratorio and operatic sopranos; whom I only got to know in her old age.

In later life I realized that my sense of tempo for a given work usually derived from Harty's performances of orchestral music, or my father's of piano music; and for lieder and French art songs, those of Helen Henschel (of whom I shall be writing later on). I might come to disagree, in the end, about a particular piece or movement, but the original tempi were clear in my mind. I think I must have been given extremely good models, for I rarely had to change my ideas because of hearing other, perhaps more famous, musicians. As the years went by, excessive speeds tended to be set, as orchestral technique improved still further (and instrumental acrobatics likewise), and as sensation seemed to supplant sobriety. Such is still the case in the 1990s! Now, at the age of over 80, I keep being reminded of my cellist uncle, Carl Fuchs who, at a similar age, refused to listen to chamber music on the radio, because "everybody plays everything too fast"!

My preparatory year was thus pretty full of activity; two lessons a week with my father, theory, and practising. I also tried my hand at composition, and wrote two string quartets. They were of course studentish and derivative (I was no genius!), but the writing gave me valuable experience which I later turned to good use as an arranger.

In the summer of 1925 all my work paid off handsomely. I took the Associated Board exam in Manchester, and won the Gold Medal for that grade. The Silver Medal was won by another Manchester student, Ida Carroll, the daughter of Walter Carroll (well-known as the composer of much piano music for children). My exam programme had included the *Partita in B flat* by J.S. Bach, Schumann's *G minor Sonata*, Fauré's *Opus 34 Impromptu in A flat*, and John Ireland's *Equinox*. There was a Graduates' Concert at which Ida and I both played. My item was the slow movement from the Schumann *Sonata*, and I was thrilled and flattered to be complimented afterwards by Dr. Brodsky himself, who said: "Now you are no longer Leonardo der Winzige (tiny) but really Leonardo da Vinci." A nice conceit, if exaggerated! That concert was also the occasion when I received a most encouraging notice (review) from the Manchester Guardian's very celebrated critic, Samuel Langford. I treasured that, and I still have it! (see Appendix; item #1)

In June I went up to London, since I had earned the right to try for a scholarship: and I got that too, so I was very happy! At the scholarship exam I saw many of the other contestants, and was impressed by the good looks and sophistication of the London girls; Manchester girls seemed dowdy by comparison! (More to look forward to in London than music, obviously!) The examiners were two men whom I got to know well in the years to come; Lloyd Powell and Arthur Benjamin, both of them good pianists (Benjamin in fact, brilliant) and most sympathetic human beings. And so, in September 1925 I was installed in London. My "digs", found for me by Aunt Christine, were on Shepherd's

Bush Green. Thus started a period of four and a half years at the Royal College of Music, where I enjoyed almost everything that was offered.

II

London

Royal College of Music

*M*Y PIANO TEACHER was Herbert Fryer (after a false start with another man who reduced me to impotence in a very few weeks, by never allowing me to play more than four consecutive bars without stopping me). Fryer was a deeply musical and non-didactic teacher whose pupils made their marks in the profession. He was not a great player himself, but he inspired many of us to work really hard. His objective was always the "musical performance" rather than merely technical proficiency. He allowed his students much freedom of choice in repertoire, and his taste was catholic enough to enable him to be of help in whatever you might bring to a lesson. His pained "How can you hurt the piano like that?" made me very aware of tone quality and of a sympathetic and springy touch. In the course of four years I went through a very considerable repertoire with Mr. Fryer: Bach and the classics, Chopin, Schumann, Brahms, Debussy, Saint-Saëns, Bloch, and more. After a year or two I formed a Sonata partnership with a pupil of Ivor James, the cellist Maurice Hardy, of whom much more is to come.

As soon as possible I started learning another instrument, the french horn, because I wanted to play in an orchestra. The College lent me a horn, and I enjoyed my lessons with Frank Probyn ("Gentleman Frank", as he was known in the profession outside). Eventually I reached the First Orchestra as fourth horn. The College at that time had three orchestras: the Third, a beginners' orchestra (otherwise known as the Jazz Band) was supervised by W.H. Reed. He was for years the concert-master of the London Symphony Orchestra and a great friend of Sir

Edward Elgar. Reed was kindly and forbearing, and the student conductors were let out on the Jazz Band from time to time. The Second
Orchestra was Malcolm Sargent's; and the First, Adrian Boult's. (They
had neither of them been knighted yet) In these two orchestras the
repertoire was very wide, and at times enormously exciting. I was
amazed to find myself playing in things like the Schubert *C major
Symphony*, the *Eroica*, the Brahms *D minor Piano Concerto*, *Wotan's
Farewell*, Mahler *IV*, or Walton's *Portsmouth Point Overture*. Members of
Dr. Sargent's conducting class (of which I was one, after a couple of
years) were encouraged to come and play percussion: that is how I came
to take part in what was, to me, a wonderful performance of Debussy's
three *Nocturnes*, under Boult. I played the cymbals, and the tiny sound
required at the end of *Fêtes* was almost beyond my powers! The cymbals
were very heavy and my hands shook so much that the things clattered.
I was saved by Boult, who suggested putting the cymbals together, silent-
ly, many bars before they were needed, and then at the right moment,
just pushing them gently apart. It worked!! (Thank goodness)

Besides studying conducting with Sargent, I took theory and composition under various people. At very first, with R.O. Morris, who was
too high-powered for my very 19th century mind; then Guy Warrack;
and finally Gordon Jacob, from whom I learnt a great deal. In the end,
Jacob was more a fatherly advisor for me than a strict teacher. In my
second year I heard Arthur Benjamin give the first performance of
Jacob's *First Piano Concerto* (the one with string orchestra) and I was immensely taken with it. I learned it as soon as I could, and performed it
under Sir Dan Godfrey in Bournemouth while I was still a student at
R.C.M. (see Appendix; item #3)

The Royal College was a very vital and exciting place in those days.
The Director, Sir Hugh Allen, was a dynamo of energy and enthusiasm;
I found him a bit terrifying, but always supportive. In some ways he was
not unlike my recent High Master at Manchester Grammar School, J.L.
Paton. Almost every kind of musical activity went on at the Royal
College of Music, at one level or another. Opera loomed large, and while
I was there I saw full productions of *Parsifal, Pelléas et Mélisande*, and *Sir
John in Love*, besides excerpts of other works. I was involved sometimes
as a horn player; later, in *Pelléas* (1928, I think) I found myself backstage

giving lighting cues for Humphrey Proctor-Gregg's complicated lighting score!

There was Ballet, run by Penelope Spencer, (whose younger sister Sylvia became an extremely good oboist under Leon Goossens). For Penelope I arranged, scored and conducted a ballet to music by Handel; I can no longer remember the scenario, or story, if there was one! I joined (maybe even helped form) a composers' group, involving such fellow students as Michael Tippett, Imogen Holst, Grace Williams, David Moule Evans and Elizabeth Maconchy. I really had no right to be there at all: my compositions were outmoded and second-hand, but I did have a set of *Variations for Orchestra* played at a Patron's Fund Concert. That, I think, showed me once and for all, that my musical mind was re-creative rather than original, and I desisted from composing, finding my pleasure in orchestrating fulfilled in other ways. But I valued the companionship of the other members of the group, and kept on seeing them and hearing their music as the years went by.

I guess I dived head first into everything that was available at the R.C.M., and made many good friends. The College life provided excitement and great satisfaction; you could meet Vaughan Williams, Gustav Holst, Herbert Howells or John Ireland in the corridors! Also pianists like Harold Samuel and Arthur Benjamin, and of course the two Big conductors, Boult and Sargent. There were concerts quite often; student recitals, informal concerts where new players or new student compositions would get their first airings, orchestral concerts; and always the possibility of giving a concerto performance. One's participation in these concerts depended upon one's own initiative plus the agreement of one's professor. I had the good fortune to appear quite often, after my first year, in solo works, chamber music, and a few times as concerto soloist. My grand finale at R.C.M. in December 1929, was to play "The Tchaikovsky" with Malcolm Sargent, and a most exhilarating occasion it was, too! I greatly admired Sargent, and he must have approved of me, since he could be cruel to concerto soloists of whom he didn't approve. Being his conducting student and a horn player under him too, certainly helped. It was a good partnership and a glorious way to finish at the R.C.M. I've never played the Tchaikovsky again; never had the chance; though a few years later on I had an equally rewarding experience of togetherness with conductor Leslie Heward and the Schumann *Concerto* in Birmingham.

During my years at the R.C.M. I made very many friends whom I should go on meeting inside the profession all the time I lived in London; some further 33 years. Many more of them found work in the provinces, so that almost wherever I went in the British Isles, I would find friends or acquaintances. And they are hard to forget: flautist John Francis, oboist Sylvia Spencer, clarinetist Wilfred Kealey, bassoonist Alf Butler, hornists Charles Gregory and John Denison (later of the Arts Council); trumpeter Cecil Kidd, who married one of the most charming girls at College, Ianthe Dalway Turnbull. Fellow pianists Kendall Taylor (my senior by a few years), Cyril Smith, Millicent Silver, Cameron Taylor, all of them also Fryer pupils; and Helen Perkin, for whom John Ireland wrote his *Piano Concerto*: composers Howard Ferguson and Robin Orr, and singers! Trefor Jones, a Welshman with a gorgeous tenor voice which he ruined singing the part of Parsifal when he was too young; Philip Ward who sang Pelléas in the R.C.M. production of Debussy's opera, and whom I shall always remember because in one performance, in the "well scene", he leaned over too far in looking for Mélisande's ring, and fell head first into the well! Then there were our two Mélisandes; Mabel Ritchie (later celebrated as Margaret Ritchie) a singer of great fastidiousness and charm; and Betty Baxendale, not as good a singer, but inordinately pretty. It was quite astonishing how many more rehearsals Betty needed than did Mabel! Dr. Sargent was indefatigable in his concern for Betty. Then there was Veronica Mansfield from Australia, and the two inseparables, Nellie Meyrat and Monica Sweeney. Oh, and the baritone Grahame Clifford, with whom a few years later I shared an apartment.

For students' relaxation there were two Common Rooms, labelled Male Students' Common Room and Female S.C.R. respectively. By 1925 these had become Smoking and Non-smoking, the latter inhabited only by girls. All my friends used the Smoking one, whether or not they were smokers. Really beautiful girls like Ruby McGilchrist and Juanita Triggs (how could I ever forget their names?!) only came to the room where the boys were. What would you expect? Once, for a bet, I took my tea into the "other room", and found myself the only male; no one spoke to me!

The College also had two lunch rooms in the basement, likewise seg-regated, though in this case the sexes did in fact separate. The men's lunch room was looked after by Doris, a jolly little woman, always good-tempered. There were maybe four tables, with places for 20 to 25 people, and there was a small hand-bell, to be used in case of need. If steak-and-kidney pie was on the menu, anyone who found a piece of kidney in his serving was entitled to ring the bell; and usually did! The supervisor of the dining rooms was a Mrs. Flowers, a buxom and motherly lady, always impeccable in a black dress and white starched apron. She presided over serving drinks to adult members of the orchestra on the occasion of opera performances (in the basement, because the Parry Opera Theatre was, in those days, also one floor down). Once, during an intermission, Mrs. Flowers was caught serving a beer (bottled Bass) to a student, which was *not allowed*. Her remonstrance became famous overnight; "Oh, Sir Hugh, what's a Bass to a wind-player?" What indeed!

One of the biggest influences in my life in those years was the friend-ship of Helen Henschel, the elder daughter of Sir George Henschel. He was the first man to sing the part of Hans Sachs in *Meistersinger* in a con-cert performance; Leipzig, 1868! Helen and my parents were friends, and my father usually stayed with Helen and her husband Harold Claughton when he came to London. Helen was a singer who played her own accompaniments (as her father had done, too) and she was a superb musician, with a great range of experience. I used, when I was allowed, to sit and listen to her practise; her repertoire ran from Elizabethan and folksongs through a great variety of lieder and French art songs, to English contemporary songs and spirituals. She was, to me, utterly com-pelling in all of them. Her voice was not a big one, but it was admirably produced, controlled and expressive throughout its range. She was a fine pianist by any standards. She had wanted to be a professional pianist, and she would play duets with me; the whole available symphonic repertoire. One Sunday morning her father, Sir George (then approaching 80 years of age) came to visit and was made to listen to us play the *Eroica*. He approved of our tempi; and so he should have, for they were his own, learned and digested by his daughter! I was quite over-awed, being in the same room with a man who had known Liszt, Anton Rubinstein and

Clara Schumann, and had been a friend of Brahms and Dvořák and Tchaikovsky. He himself was kindly and wise. A year or two later I went to him for coaching; with his younger daughter Georgie (Georgina was her full name; she was, like her sister, a soprano) and with my cellist partner from R.C.M., Maurice Hardy.

Helen was roughly the same age as my parents, so at that time was in her early forties. She was beautiful and glamorous, and I regarded her as a sort of musical fairy god-mother; and I learnt a great deal from her about music of all sorts, from Dowland to Gershwin. I also found in her a ready listener to my youthful troubles; though she rarely solved them! But when one has been absolutely bowled over by hearing, and seeing, *Parsifal* two and a half times in two weeks (into the bargain one's first introduction to the music), and one is only 17; one needs someone to whom one can come and unload, as I did. Altogether I feel I owe her and her father an enormous debt, in that they made me more than ever aware of the meaning of music and of musical integrity.

After those formative years I saw Helen but rarely, but I knew her before she became totally obsessed with her father's life and accomplishments. She would say: "You know what Father said about...?" rather as J.L.Paton used to say "and what did St. Paul have to say about this?" St. Paul, bless him, always had something to say about everything!

None the less, for some four years, Helen Henschel was a fairy-godmother to me. She had me give her two children, Peter and Joan, piano lessons, and I used sometimes to take Joan, aged 8, to the Robert Mayer Childrens' Concerts, where Malcolm Sargent conducted, and captivated his young audiences. If Joan sometimes played lumpily or unrhythmically at a lesson, I had only to say "imagine Dr. Sargent doing this", and it would miraculously come right. Such is the power of personality projection; Joan felt it from Malcolm Sargent, and I from her mother. But this was not calf-love; it was hero-worship. There are still some songs; Brahms' *Von Ewiger Liebe*, Schumann's *Widmung*, Debussy's *Chevaux de Bois;* which I can never hear, after 60 years, without thinking of her and hearing her voice, and her tempo, and her expressiveness. Helen also introduced me to the lighter side of music, which she enjoyed to the full: unlike my father, who could scarcely abide even Sullivan, and who felt debauched and dirtied by hearing jazz or even good Gershwin. I was, and still am, sorry for him. I made the acquaintance of *An American in Paris* when it was quite new in 1928, and found it enchanting; and *Tiger Rag*, and *Tea for Two*. They were all new and delicious. The show *No, No, Nanette* I saw in its original production, also 1928. Thus, more sides of music than the severely classical, upon which I had been brought up, were opened to me. Dieu merçi!

In fairness to my family, I should add that Helen Henschel was not the only influence, musical or otherwise, in my life at this time. I did have an uncle and two aunts, plus three cousins living in London then!

Uncle Alf and Aunt Rose were both doctors, as I have said, brother and sister respectively of my mother. Alf's wife Christine was a violinist; and many a Sunday evening was spent at their Wimpole Street house, listening to chamber music of all kinds; with and without piano. Very occasionally I was asked to join in, but mostly I was audience or page-turner for the others. Here also I learnt a lot of music which is hardly, if at all, played nowadays: Pierné and Florent Schmitt *Piano Quintets*, the Fauré *Piano Quartets* and *Quintets*, Franck, Roger-Ducasse, Chausson, Lekeu. They explored the French repertoire, and the playing seemed to me to be quite admirable. Aunt Rose was the only Jordan relative who proclaimed herself *un*-musical, yet it was she who, after listening to me play the Brahms *G minor Rhapsody, opus 79 #2*, said to me, "How can you call yourself a pacifist and yet play a piece like that?!"

Certainly, in those days, we teenagers would be pacifist; passionately hoping the League of Nations would be successful, and hating the Kiplingesque "patriots" who still beat drums and waved the Union Jack. Of course, we were to be very sadly disillusioned before many more years passed, and our disgust with Neville Chamberlain and the other "appeasers" was all the greater. In the meantime we hoped that Austen Chamberlain, Briand and Stresemann would be able to pull Europe out of its awful mess and muddle. For most of us, though, our pacifism disappeared with the coming of Hitler.

During my first years in London there were two other families in whose company I spent a lot of time. One was named Eichholz. Dr. Eichholz had been a Cambridge friend of my Uncle Alf, and their friendship had continued through the years since university. Alfred Eichholz, when I knew him, was Chief Medical Inspector for the Board of Education; his special interests were the schools for blind and deaf children. He was a man of great intelligence and high principles, with a most delightful sense of humour. I did not meet his like again until some forty years later, when I met Dr. Samuel Freedman, the Chief Justice of Manitoba. Dr. Eichholz's wife, Ruth, was the daughter of the late Chief Rabbi of England, Herz, and she was as fine a human being as her husband. For me they were not only friends, and when required, mentors too; they exemplified the finest type of Jewish couple. They were wholly cultivated and lovable people, and I admired them very much. Of their three sons, the youngest, David, was the nearest to me in age. He was a classical scholar; and during a holiday trip to Persia he contracted polio. In those days there seemed nothing at all which could be done to alleviate this horror, and David spent the rest of his life in a wheelchair. None the less, he filled the position of Professor of Classics at Bristol University, and lived an astonishingly full life. We used to meet relatively often, especially during the earlier part of the 1939 - 1945 war, when I too lived in Bristol.

The other family of whom I saw a good deal during my student years (and subsequently too) lived on the edge of London, at Kew, where the lovely Botanical Gardens are. Neville Smith was London correspondent of the Manchester Guardian. He and his wife and my parents had become acquainted when they lived opposite each other in the small Manchester street where I was born; so indeed I had known them for as long as I had been alive! Margaret Smith, for some reason always known as Auntie Peter (probably because of her shock of hair as a young woman, recalling Struwwelpeter; "Shock-headed Peter") became for me a mother-figure. She was a reservoir of wisdom and kindness of which I was apt to be in some real need at times. Their three children, Nora, John and Mary (Polly) became great friends of mine; for some time I taught John music and he was a very apt pupil. In the later 1920's (I forget which actual year) Neville Smith died very suddenly, and I found that in a small degree I was able to be a help and support to his widow and her children. My visits to Kew were very special to me, and I loved the whole Smith family. Auntie Peter and the Eichholz family taught me a great deal about integrity and intellectual honesty, and I continued to see Auntie Peter long after my student days were over; she lived to be well over 90.

My appetite for travel, which had been whetted by the Spanish trip in the summer of 1924, was given a great boost two years later by a continental summer holiday. My mother, sister Ruth and I, along with Uncle Carl and Aunt Nelly Fuchs and their elder son Arnold, went for a stay in Alsace, and then a journey into Germany. The Alsatian visit was quite lovely; a tiny village called Dabo (in German "Dagsburg", which form my uncle insisted on using). The village was set among low hills, with a little church on the top of the nearest one: its Sunday morning bells were a delight. There was the constant smell of wood-fires, carefully blazoned walks through the woods, and a very nice clean hotel. My French was good enough for general conversation, and I had a wonderful time. I remember a family of Dutch people who were also staying there; Dr. Schreve and his three children and two sisters-in-law. I promptly fell in love with his daughter Frida, who was my own age: that was the first time such a thing happened to me, though not the last!

After Dabo we went on to Strasbourg, and thence down the Rhine to Wesel-am-Rhein, where we had relatives. At least part of the way, from Bingen to Bonn, we travelled by boat. On the way we met with Cousin Dr. Carl Zaudy, and in Wesel we stayed with the Brandenstein family. Hugo Brandenstein's wife was a Zaudy, so we were cousins of some sort! Sad to say, all the Zaudys and Brandensteins who didn't manage to get to England or America, after 1933 disappeared from the face of the earth. There were Zaudys in Berlin too. All gone.

Somewhere in this journey we visited a little place near Darmstadt called Jugenheim-an-der-Bergstrasse. Here lived Great-uncle Franz Loewenthal and Uncle Carl Fuchs's sister Wally. Uncle Franz, though he'd lived near Manchester for years, had never bothered to become a naturalized English citizen. He was therefore interned by the English in 1915; then at the end of the war was sent back to Germany. He and Tante Wally joined forces, and their small incomes, and lived there contentedly for several years. Ironically, Uncle Carl and his family had been caught in Germany by the outbreak of war in 1914. He, along with Edgar Bainton, Benjamin Dale, Ernest MacMillan and others, was interned in Ruhleben by the Germans. When the German authorities discovered that Uncle Carl had done his military training in the German army years earlier, they let him out of Ruhleben, but not out of the country: that had to wait until 1919. By the summer of 1926 when we were visiting in Germany, there seemed little rancour left in the small places we stayed in. I felt very much at home there, as I did in Berlin in 1930.

However, I have digressed considerably!

My finish at the R.C.M. was in December 1929. Looking back, I think we were very lucky to be students in London in those particular years. We certainly worked hard, but we were not under the somewhat excessive pressure which besets music students in the 1990s; universities requiring courses in non-practical subjects, throughout a 4-year pro-gramme; thus taking time away from learning one's means of making music, i.e. instrument or voice. For us, in the 1920s, making music came first, but I somehow still had time to prepare for the theory and history examinations of the London University Bachelor of Music Degree. The History I read in my own time, since there was no instruction in the subject at the R.C.M. It seemed to matter little. I heard and saw a lot, including the Promenade Concerts, opera, and ballet. I was still in time to see the Diaghilev Ballet in its last year; Woizikowski in *Tricorne*, and *Petrouchka*. There were the opera productions at the R.C.M.; up in the "gods" at Covent Garden; and I especially remember the Chaliapin-Beecham production of *Boris Godunov*.

I also remember the day Vaughan Williams brought Ravel, very natti-ly dressed in a mauve suit and pointed yellow shoes, into the R.C.M. Concert Hall to hear us rehearsing his *Daphnis and Chloe* under Adrian Boult: and the day I played Beethoven *Opus 110* to Myra Hess in the course of some competition for a gold medal. I think I won it that year; and Myra remembered my Beethoven, for she referred to it many years later. The whole period was in fact a "fine time" to which I look back with deep pleasure and some nostalgia.

≡III≡
Paris and Berlin

Now, in January of 1930, I needed some new experience and different teaching; and my father's old friend Alfred Cortot accepted me for the École Normale de Musique in Paris. It became a question of how to manage it financially, for my father's blindness had greatly decreased his earning capacity. During all my time at the R.C.M. we had been helped by the City of Manchester Education Committee, and by Dad's family; notably his brother-in-law Alec Jacobs and his cousin in New York, Harry Scherman, the owner of the Book-of-the-Month Club. Cortot offered me a scholarship, so the expenses were solely those of day to day living. A one-time student of Dad's lived in Paris, married to a Turkish jeweller named Soulam. Their apartment was in a very nice part of Paris, Avenue du President Wilson; and she found a room for me almost next-door, with some cousins of her husband's. I hired a small Pleyel upright, and I was set for the next six months.

In the apartment where I lived were the widowed Madame Abeles (Hungarian by marriage), her sister Mlle. Béhar (Italian, I think), and an elderly gentleman cousin Monsieur Frescaut. The ladies were lively, M. Frescaut quiet and courteous, and the other occupant was the little "bonne à tout faire", Rosa, who cleaned and cooked (both Madame and her sister worked). On Sundays we would all meet for lunch; and each Sunday I would notice a particularly delicious odour as the Sunday dinner was cooking. It was a scent quite new to me, and one day I summoned up enough courage to ask Rosa what she was using. It turned out to be garlic, against which my mother had warned me in the most serious way. She said it was an *awful* taste and stank the place out! I decided her warning had been quite wrong, and have eaten garlic with pleasure ever since!

Most Sunday evenings we were all invited over to the Soulam's for a meal; these were wild occasions! There were four Soulams, Monsieur, Madame and 2 children; there were M. Soulam's greatest friends, also Turkish, called Rosannès, three of them; there might also be Monsieur and Madame Lévy from downstairs; and the four of us from next door. French was spoken mostly, but if the gentlemen wanted to talk business they went off into Arabic; they also would speak Spanish every now and then for Madame Lévy's sake, who was Spanish. Just occasionally a word in English would be pronounced for my benefit! If you wanted something to eat, you reached out across the table with your fork and speared it! The first time we went there, I was too shy and well-mannered to stretch out, and I got nothing to eat at all! By the second visit I had learnt. The noise was indescribable, but *so* good-tempered. Hitler's Germans did away with all of them, too.

On weekdays no one cooked in my apartment. I found a little restaurant behind the Etoile; some ten minutes' walk away; and became a "regular" there. I was promoted to my own serviette, and was known as Monsieur Trente-Sept; that was the number of the napkin! I became fascinated by an enormously fat lady whom I often saw there. One day I found myself at the same table with her: she turned out to be an Irishwoman, married to a M. Laverne, and we became good friends.

As in London, I worked hard, but Paris proved a lonely place at times in spite of my two "families". As my French improved I made some friendships, one or two of which lasted well. I had the joy of a few lessons with Cortot himself, and played accompaniments for the Casals students. Casals knew my Uncle Carl Fuchs and welcomed me. He was a courteous and kindly teacher, and we wondered why he allowed his disciple Diran Alexanian to harm so many young cellists with his inflexible methods. Nevertheless, Alexanian's chamber music class was invigorating. Each member was set one movement of a chamber work: I won the *Pantoum* from the Ravel *Piano Trio*, and felt that the whole reputation of English piano-playing was on my shoulders! (Luckily the performance went well; Alexanian was almost complimentary about it!)

I was the only English student; the others came from Romania, Bulgaria, Finland, Switzerland and France itself, in the person of a charming girl named Pauline Barbé[9]. She could sing Chopin's *F minor Etude opus 25* in solfège, at the correct speed; a great party-trick which she was often called upon to demonstrate.

In Paris there was much to see and hear; *Pelléas* at the Opéra Comique, the great clown Grock at the Salle Wagram; Pavlova at the Grand Opéra; symphony concerts in the Salle Pleyel and the Châtelet, where Monteux or Wolff were conducting. At the Salle Pleyel I heard Ravel's *Bolero* for the first time; the rest of the audience were also clearly hearing it for the first time too, and were at first non-plussed! Then they became by turns uncomfortable, engrossed and finally, enthusiastic. The audiences generally were not quite as docile and well-behaved as in London. I remember a performance of Tchaikovsky #6 when, in the pause after the third movement, a little man in the balcony jumped up and shouted at the top of his voice "Pourquoi jouez-vous ce sale-prix? Pourquoi pas de Schubert?" No one paid any attention!

Work at the École Normale included some student concerts, at one or two of which I played. The first time I played, it was to be Debussy's *Reflets dans l'eau*. I set out to walk to the École, but I got a cinder in my eye which I simply could not dislodge. I had to play with the tears still streaming down onto the keyboard (which provided the reflets), but no one seemed to notice!

Nadia Boulanger was on faculty there, but my ignorance was abysmal: I'd no idea who she was! So I missed out on a series of lectures she gave on Brahms. I thought I knew about him and needed no French lecturer to tell me! Years later I met Nadia at the BBC and realized what a fool I'd been.

At the end of my time there I attended Cortot's spring *Cours d'Interprétation*; an unforgettable journey through the piano works of Debussy, during which we students played selected pieces and received a public lesson on them. And then too, I had the thrilling experience of playing the César Franck *Variations Symphoniques* with Cortot himself playing the second piano for me!

During my stay in Paris I made the acquaintance, through an introduction given me by Herbert Howells, of that great lady Louise Dyer, the founder of the Lyre-Bird Press (Les Editions de L'Oiseau-Lyre). At her and her husband's apartment I actually met and played to Madame Debussy. *Oh!* I was scared, and did not play too well. Mrs. Dyer was an Australian (her brother was Lord Mayor of Melbourne); chez Dyer you could meet any Australian artist or musician who was visiting Paris. Their apartment was lavishly modern, and very comfortable indeed. The dining room, as far as I can remember now, was black and a beautiful pastel shade of green, and the table decoration was a huge cubic bowl of live fish! Jimmie Dyer did not fit into this Parisian style with any ease. He was a Scotsman who'd settled in Australia many years previously; made a fortune in linoleum, and then dutifully followed his wife to Paris, which he disliked intensely. However, it was they together who took me to see Pavlova. Mrs. Dyer was always beautifully gowned; you couldn't just call it "dressed". For me it was a quite exceptional experience to follow her and Jimmie up the great staircase at the Grand Opéra, with everyone looking at Louise and wondering who she might be. Of course, I never addressed either of them by their first names. But I became very fond of Mrs. Dyer, and of Mr. too, in a funny, dour way! I thought she was too innocent to manage some of the curiously thoughtless treatment she was accorded by one or two of her editors. She used to complain to me about what they did to her, which I fear I didn't properly understand. As a thank you for all the kindnesses which she had shown me, I invited her out to dinner (or was it lunch?). She actually accepted, and I took immense pains to order a meal which I thought worthy of her; including "fraises de bois" (wild strawberries) which I still think are the most delicate and rare fruits one can eat!

At the end of my six months in Paris I was longing to get to Germany to complete the year abroad, but I had no money for such a project. Mrs. Dyer found out about my ambition and gave me 50 pounds (which was in those days a princely sum) enabling me to go to Berlin. I was speechlessly grateful for such kindness, and when she and Jimmie came to Berlin in the fall I played for them. Hopefully they felt their generosity had been worthwhile!

In Berlin my father's contacts again helped me: an old friend and former Busoni pupil, Michael Zadora, found me lodgings in the Duisburgerstrasse, with a friendly family named Baumann. Sadly, they all disappeared after 1933, along with the aforementioned Berlin Zaudy's. They were all Jewish; so much for the godforsaken fools who deny the reality of the Holocaust. These were all good and harmless people, unlike the present day anti-semites and racial "purists".

For piano lessons in Berlin I went to Egon Petri, maybe the foremost Busoni disciple. Petri lived in Zakopane, Poland, and taught in Berlin every couple of weeks. For teaching he used Busoni's old apartment, where Frau Busoni was still living and where Busoni's pianos still were. In the music room was a bust of Busoni and a cast of his hands. It was almost too much for me: the intense face, a little like the gaze of Beethoven; the dark-coloured, bronze cast hands and the very instruments those hands had played on! The room was full of his spirit; and the man I was auditioning for had been his favourite pupil. Petri had been on the staff of the Royal Manchester College of Music when I was born, and most certainly remembered my parents, if not me myself. I was completely over-awed by all this, and played abominably! Luckily for me, he still accepted me as a student, at a reduced price of 50 marks. Petri only charged the larger sum of 100 marks per lesson because Artur Schnabel also did, but he said, "I only ever get it from rich Americans!"

I had enough money for six lessons. They were roughly two and a half hours long, and I was both spent and exhilarated at the end of each one; hurrying home to try and recapture what we had been doing before I could possibly forget it. I learned more about actually playing the piano in those three months than in all the time leading up to them, though when I got home to Manchester and told my parents what Petri had said, Dad replied, "I used to tell you that too, but you were too young then to understand!"

I had some friends of my own age in Berlin; a couple of them who had also been in Paris. Paul Schoop, who was now in Hindemith's film-music class at the Hochschule; and Anna Drittel, the Russian cellist I knew in Paris. Anna's family were very Russian and could have come straight out of a Chekhov story. There was an American called Steve Lewis, and a couple of others who made up a friendly group. Together we went to see *Götterdämmerung*, all of us for the first time. For the price of 2 marks each, we stood at the back of the gallery for five hours! Afterwards, exhausted, we went for some supper of spaghetti and chianti;

and I walked all the way home, my feet never touching the pavement!!

Among other operas I saw in Berlin were *Prince Igor, Fidelio*, and *Tristan* (with Emmy Heim as Isolde); and the *Dreigroschenoper*, then new, which I found distasteful and unsettling, as one was supposed to! I also saw, twice, an enchanting folk-story opera by Weinberger, *Schwanda the Bagpiper*, of which most people now know only the *Polka* and *Fugue*. A pity it's not staged any longer; it is tuneful and effective.

There was a tremendous performance of the *Eroica*, under Klemperer, who was then the conductor at the Kroll Opera. It was so forceful that I crawled away afterwards, not daring to present him with the introduction Sargent had given me! And then I didn't meet him until many years later. Also I well remember a beautiful Brahms *F minor Sonata* played by Edwin Fischer, which sent me scurrying down to Bote und Bock next morning for a copy of the music. It was then quite new to me, and I spent a lot of time learning it; but not with Petri, who told me he disliked the work. How is that possible?!

At a recital given by Petri himself I met another of his students, an American named Louis Crowder, who subsequently went on to work with Claudio Arrau, and who ended up a respected University teacher in the U.S.

While I was in Berlin, several of my older friends passed through on their way elsewhere: one member of a family I knew in London, Mary Manson, whose father had been Curator of the Tate Gallery; Imogen Holst and Grace Williams, both of whom I took to see *Schwanda*. I think Grace enjoyed it, but it was not nearly highbrow enough for Imogen, who merely tolerated it!

One weekend I made a pilgrimage to Leipzig, to see Bach's church and the musical instrument museum. At the museum I made friends with one of the attendants, who got various ancient horns out of their cases for me to try and blow. But I was not allowed to touch Bach's harpsichord; it was locked into a glass case. The visit to the Thomaskirche on Sunday morning was disappointing, because what was performed during Service was a *Cantata* by Arnold Mendelssohn. This was, for me at least, a very poor substitute for the Bach I had hoped to hear. The Turm-musik, however, played on brass instruments from the top of St. Nicholas' tower, was thrilling in the bright morning sunshine.

Other performances I remember from Berlin include my first hearing of *Mahler #5*, the Brahms *Requiem* (which I knew very well indeed from having played in it, several times, under Arnold Goldsbrough at St. Martin-in-the-Fields), and the *Missa Solemnis*. The last time I'd heard that was in Paris, in the Madeleine, where it had been treated as a religious service; they had rung a little bell through most of the Offertorium, which I thought a bit unsuitable!

The three months in Berlin came to an end, and I made my journey home via Jugenheim, in order to see Franz Loewenthal and Tante Wally again. I've always been very glad I did so, for I never saw either of them after that. We had a Christmas visit; they were very kind and hospitable. I was very proud that my 21 years were acknowledged by my being offered a cigar, even if I couldn't smoke it with any real enjoyment! And so in 1930, my student years over, I came back to England all set to try and earn my living as a professional musician, but without any job in sight.

During the years I had so far spent in London (1925 - 1929), I had lived in only two sets of "digs". The first, in Shepherd's Bush, only lasted one year! The landlady there was fussy, and a poor, unimaginative cook; too much finnan haddock! She had a rather henpecked husband who was garrulous when permitted, and a young and silly daughter Pauline, who used to practise "Ukelele Lady" on their out-of-tune piano, with the door open, when she knew full well that I was trying to work at harmony exercises upstairs! I had a small Dale Forty piano in my small room, and in fairness to the landlady, none of her family complained about my practising, so I couldn't in decency complain about Pauline's. It was here, too, that I started to break in my french horn, and I suppose it was pretty gruesome. One day an anonymous note was pushed through the letter-box. It said *"Will the person kindly give us a rest from those grunting perforances* (sic) *on the voilin* (sic). *If we want music we know where to get it."* The last jab was particularly snide, since the Shepherd's Bush Empire, a music-hall, was just next door! I did not desist, and gradually the horn playing got better.

The autumn of that first year (1925) the Lener String Quartet from Hungary played in London, and I was allowed backstage to hear their concerts without paying. My father had brought them to Manchester

the previous year for their first appearance in England, and notwith-
standing their somewhat primitive English, we had all become good
friends. The most approachable of the four was Joseph Smilovits, the
second violin; although the others, Jeno Lener, a rather awe-inspiring
character, Sandor Roth and Imre Hartmann were all equally friendly,
and all four were most beautiful players. Lener's violin was one of two
Spanish Strads, with mother-of-pearl purfling, and it sang divinely. They
were a great quartet and became immensely popular in London. From
them I really learned the classical quartet repertoire, from Haydn to
Debussy, Ravel and Kodaly. By that date Bartok had only written one of
his eventual six quartets; but that too was already in their repertoire. At
one of their concerts in the Wigmore Hall, there was an occurrence
which I had never before witnessed, nor since either. In the middle of
the last movement of Beethoven *Opus 132*, the second violin's A string
broke, but they did not stop. Smilovits finished the quartet on the three
strings he had left! By the end he was dripping with perspiration, but he
succeeded!

During that season also, I made the acquaintance of a cousin of
Smilovits, a young man called John Tannert. John was in business, but
was also a keen amateur violinist. We got together pretty regularly that
year, and ploughed our way through most of Mozart, Beethoven, Grieg
and Brahms piano and violin sonatas, and also part of my father's sonata,
which we played to him on one of his visits to London.

In the new year (1926) a new lodger arrived at my digs; a Scot from
Dunfermline named Jim Barber, with a basso profundo voice, who was
also studying at the Royal College. We became great friends (he taught
me to smoke; a habit which I only kicked 63 years later!), and after a
while we were out together looking for a new and pleasanter place to
live for the following academic year. We moved out to Bedford Park, a
western suburb on the way to Kew and Richmond; a very pleasant district. We found two places in the same road, each of which had room for
one student, and we stayed in Bedford Park for the rest of our time at
college. I was happy in these digs; the family consisted of an elderly
mother, two unmarried daughters of "uncertain" age, and a bachelor
son. There were other lodgers too, but no one ever complained about
my practising. In the course of time, Mrs. Kemp took in other music stu-

dents, a clarinetist and a soprano, and I knew them both. Wilfred Kealey's clarinet was bearable, but Jo Ashley's piercing vocal practise was very disturbing! I found it hard to endure, and little thought that within a few years I should be sharing an apartment with a singer; albeit a baritone!

Of the non-musical people who also lived at the Kemp's while I was there (it was a big house) I specially remember two most civilized Siamese students, Xuto and Ranong, who were charming and friendly. One of them was a medical student and the other a veterinarian. A story they told has stayed with me all these years. They had gone for a day's outing to Brighton for some sea air, and hopefully some sunshine, and while there, on the top deck of a bus, they saw a very pretty girl sitting with an elderly woman. They commented in their own language on the girl and her looks; and were paralyzed when her companion turned around and addressed them, in Siamese! I think they dismounted at the next stop!

But this is again a long digression. I had come back from Germany at the end of 1930, needing somewhere to live. My previous digs in Bedford Park would be rather too far out of town, so I found a room in Earl's Court, in the apartment of a retired Indian Army Major, Sale-Hill and his wife. From this base I hoped to make my living, but it was very slow! I remember little about the first months of 1931 except working again with Maurice Hardy, my cellist partner from R.C.M., and preparing a recital programme for a concert we hoped to give at Leighton House in Kensington. I think we gave it in 1931, though certainly we gave another there later. We played together until 1936 and had a reasonable repertoire of Sonatas which we performed from memory; Beethoven *F major, G minor and A major* (later the *C major*), Brahms *E minor*, Debussy and Kodaly. Later, we also learned Mendelssohn *D major*, and (*not* from memory) Bach *Nos. 1 and 2*. Looking back on our performances from this distance, I think they must have been really quite good, and certainly musical. I know that when we later ventured into the Wigmore Hall, we received an extremely warm and complimentary 'notice' from the redoubtable Ernest Newman, of which we were very proud. (see Appendix; item #9)

≡IV≡

1931: "Merrie England" Goes to Canada

*I*N 1931 THINGS didn't go too well financially and I cannot any longer remember what I lived on; maybe my father! In the summer I received a telephone call from a singer I had known at R.C.M., Leyland White, who was the fiancé of Jo Ashley, the piercing soprano from my former digs. He asked if I'd like to go to Canada with a touring light opera company which needed a coach and pianist. This sounded wonderful. I had no experience as an opera coach, but I sure was prepared to try. At Leyland's arranging I went to meet the conductor and was given the job. Rehearsals would start in September, and the tour bookings began in the early winter. The conductor was a little North-country man (like me!) called Henry Jaxon who had been with the music publishing firm of Ascherberg Hopwood and Crewe for many years. He turned out to be a pretty weak conductor, but the only times I got to conduct in Canada were when he had had a 'drop too much' and couldn't!

At first I was rather shy at rehearsals, until I discovered that I knew as much about music as anyone else there. We were to play *Merrie England*, with quite charming music by Edward German, and the *Beggar's Opera*. I had grown up on Gilbert and Sullivan in Manchester and especially in London: Sargent's famous Princes Theatre season was marvelous, when he was at last permitted to use Sullivan's original and very beautiful scores. Basil Hood and Edward German were not equal in any way to Gilbert and Sullivan, but *Merrie England* had some wit, some movement, a little excitement, and a few really good songs. Jaxon made all the arrangements for the 18th century tunes for the *Beggar's Opera*, in order to avoid paying copyright fees on the Frederick Austin version. These new harmonizations of Jaxon's often offended my rather pedantic taste, and I contrived to alter those I found the most infelicitous.

There were 16 of us altogether in the company; we were to tour Canada from Montreal to Victoria, and pick up a fresh chorus in each town. These choruses would have already learned their notes, but it was to be my job and that of a Miss Evans (whose first name I forget) to lick them into 'stage shape' a day or so before each opening night. And that, in fact, is how it went; and pretty successfully too, thanks to the Canadian chorus trainers.

Our rehearsals in London over, we embarked on the *S.S. Laurentic* for Montreal; conductor, producer John Redmond, stage manager Mr. Whittle, pianist, and the company. This consisted of a rather odd mixture of types; operatic, musical comedy, concert party, light opera, straight concert; a really mixed bag of singers. We started out in fine spirits and got along together pretty well most of the way; little knowing what was in store for us a few weeks down the road.

I have no recollection of playing in Montreal; I suppose we did; but I do remember meeting, and greatly liking the music critic William Archer. I also remember a party at some club at which I was unwise enough to drink a "bottled cocktail" (a quite terrible drink which more or less laid me out). Those were the days of Prohibition; so I have no idea of the composition of the drink. I know that at about 3 a.m. I wandered over to a piano and tried to play the Albeniz *Tango*, but I could see 6 black notes where there should have been 3; and so I gave up in disgust. I have no idea how I got back to the hotel!

In Toronto I saw an R.C.M. friend, Ettore Mazzoleni, who had recently been sent out by Sir Hugh Allen to teach music at Upper Canada College. Ettore eventually became head of the Conservatory of Music in Toronto. When I saw him he had a smashing little sports car in which he drove one or two of us around at breakneck speed! Of the Royal Alex Theatre, at which we played, I can remember nothing.

We played in Ottawa, and I do remember that performance! The old Russell Theatre was uncomfortable and dirty. In Fort William (as it then still was) we played with hardly any orchestra. Indeed, for the matinee of the *Beggar's Opera*, only a clarinet turned up and there was no part for him. So we sent him home, and I played the whole show on the piano!

Then, always moving by train, we reached Winnipeg and the snow; my first ice-hockey game (as spectator, naturally), and a really great chorus. They were trained by one John McTaggart, a big tall man, as I remember him, with very thick glasses. We played in the Walker Theatre (later for many years an Odeon Cinema) to good audiences and an enthusiastic reception. And here I was allowed to conduct a performance of *Merrie England*; after all, I had been engaged as 'deputy conductor'. Our Welsh tenor tried all he could to throw me in *Dan Cupid hath a Garden* but I was used to playing *Danny Boy* for him, and I knew his style of rubato. I was angry though, that he tried such a trick on me at a performance. He didn't do it again!

Winnipeg was exciting. To this rather staid young Englishman it all seemed a bit like living inside an American movie; especially the ice-hockey game, with its loud-speakers blaring jazz during the intervals of play, and everyone chewing gum! A group of us was taken in tow by some of the chorus, and we had a wonderful time for those two weeks. When I came back to Winnipeg to live, 30-odd years later, I could find only one member of our 1931 chorus still around. Her name was Ena Scott. I remember her with great pleasure; a young married woman with a charming husband, a new house and piano, and great zest for life. Bernard Naylor had not yet arrived in Winnipeg to conduct the Philharmonic Choir, but when we came back on our return journey, he was there; another of my R.C.M. acquaintances. And he was back there again when I moved to Winnipeg in 1963.

After our two weeks in Winnipeg we moved on to Regina, which was another high spot. We played in Darke Hall, then only two years old; our chorus had been trained by the celebrated Dan Cameron, and it was first-rate, needing very little work on our parts to make it stage-worthy. I remember particularly the vivacious Cecilia Eddy and her brother Otis, who both turned up later in London. The visit ended with a terrific party on stage, and it was a contented company which made the next dates in Saskatoon, Edmonton and Calgary. Another, rather wild, party in the Macdonald Hotel ended the Edmonton days: I fear we scandalized the place with our noise! In Calgary the theatre's resident violinist was that splendid player Jean de Rimanocsy. We made some music together (other than Edward German and Dr. Pepusch) and he introduced me, very belatedly, to Gershwin's *Rhapsody in Blue.*

I very much enjoyed travelling by the CPR and seeing the huge locomotives which pulled the trains across the continent; they were still of course steam locomotives with personalities, like *Pacific 231,* and not yet the sexless diesel engines. The enjoyment became a positive thrill as we climbed through the Rockies on our way to Vancouver. The customary stop at the Great Divide allowed time for photographs, the air was cold and fresh-smelling. I made friends with one of the engine-drivers, but it was in vain that I begged for a ride on the foot-plate! In Edmonton I had seen, for the first time, rows of houses decorated with Christmas lights, a beautiful and quite moving sight; and from the train we caught glimpses of small places similarly bedecked. Vancouver was an awe-inspiring city, set as it was between such formidable mountains and the Pacific Ocean. All seemed set for a good two weeks. And then our nemesis overtook us.

Merrie England was all right, but it seemed that *Beggar's Opera* had already been played there that same season by Alfred Heather's company, and we had not been warned. So, at less than a week's notice, we had to mount a totally different show! Mr. Jaxon just happened to have with him the complete material of *Cavalleria Rusticana* (an Ascherberg, Hopwood and Crewe publication!) and some of *Faust.* So we set to; cast *Cav* and the Garden Scene from *Faust* as best suited our company, and rehearsed every day and all day when we were not actually playing *Merrie England.* Some sort of scenery and costumes were discovered. Mr. Jaxon coached *Cav* and I did *Faust.* We had one orchestral rehearsal (a band of nine plus me on the piano) and no dress rehearsals.

The new show opened with Rossini's *Semiramide* Overture, then *Faust* which went not too badly considering all things. And then, after intermission, came *Cavalleria Rusticana.* All went well until we came to the Easter Hymn. Then, with everyone kneeling on stage, we realized that there was no instrument to play the organ cues, and no backstage chorus to sing the Hymn! Mr. Jaxon had forgotten about them! There was maybe 20 seconds' of dead silence (it seemed like hours!) and then I started to play the Hymn on the piano. On stage, our Santuzza jumped

in and sang the soprano line; somehow or other we joined up with ourselves and the opera carried on, a bit shakily. By the next night I had
cued in the organ bits into the wind parts, but the conductor cut the
whole thing. It was disastrous, and our audiences didn't turn up. We
played to half-empty houses, and at the end of the week our backers, two
brothers from Montreal, took what was in the box office and decamped
back to the East. We never saw them again. We were stranded.

This has happened to touring companies over and over again, so
maybe we had all been a bit too sanguine; not making adequate
enquiries about the Montreal chaps, especially in the middle of the Great
Depression. But there was little use crying; there we were, thousands of
miles from home, with hardly any money, and the remaining weeks of
our tour apparently killed. I never knew who it was who managed to
arrange for us to continue, and fulfil the theatre bookings which had
been made for the return trip. We went on to Victoria to play one week
there; and I suffered the ignominy of being turned out of the dining
room of the Empress Hotel! We had been in the habit of signing cheques
for our meals against the takings in the box office, but, unknown to me,
the Hotel had cancelled the arrangement. Having eaten my dinner, I was
prepared to sign the cheque, but was firmly escorted into the foyer. The
producer had to send someone to the theatre to get the price of my
meal, while he himself stayed as hostage; and I *ran* to the theatre and
tumbled into the orchestra pit on the conductor's first down-beat!

We went back to Vancouver, wondering what was to become of us.
And then a very sporting and courageous decision was made, presum-
ably by Mr. Jaxon and the producer John Redmond. Mr. Jaxon had in
his rather voluminous luggage the script of a pantomime, *Sinbad the
Sailor,* as it had been played at the Theatre Royal, Leeds, in 1907 or
thereabouts. They decided to bring the script up to date, mount it, and
try to play our way back across Canada. An English pantomime is a most
curious production; it rarely has anything to do with the title under
which it operates. It's a Christmas-time show, and is completely topsy-
turvy. The hero, the Principal Boy, is played by a girl; the heroine is the
Principal Girl; there is usually an Emperor and a King of the Genies (or
Devils); and a troupe of comedians headed by the character known as
the Dame (or Widow Twankey) who is really the central figure in the

pantomime, and who is always played by a man! There is virtually no plot, but at the end, Boy gets Girl, the Emperor is made to look foolish, and the Dame ends, as 'she' began, the centrepiece of the show. The music is mostly of well-known popular favourites, either current or old-time, with a ballet or other spectacular showpiece thrown in somewhere, for good measure.

So, living in the Vancouver Hotel on credit, against our probable (or possible) takings, we spent three weeks over Christmas 1931 to New Year's 1932 constructing *Sinbad the Sailor.* The girls sewed and cut, and turned *Merrie England* and *Beggar's Opera* costumes into Pantomime wear. Mr. Redmond, Mr. Whittle and the stage carpenter chopped up and re-painted the scenery; and the company was wholly re-cast. Dorothy Crofts, our Musical Comedy girl, was to be Principal Boy; Mollie Elvar, the little Polly Peacham, became Principal Girl; the Producer became the Dame; Leyland White, our straight baritone, had become the Emperor of China; some of the minor members took on second-string comedy rôles; our Welsh tenor, disguised as a Sheik, covered his arms and face with brown guck and sang *You Are My Heart's Delight* to the audience at large; and the conductor and I spent night after night arranging all kinds of numbers (some of them, I fear, still in copyright) straight into the band parts. Finally, our pantomime was ready and rehearsed, and with great hopes on our parts, the curtain went up on *Sinbad the Sailor, 1932 version.* People came to see what a Pantomime might in fact be. They had a good evening's entertainment, some pleasant music, some good singing (and some not so good), and an inspired bit of clowning by John Redmond, who enjoyed himself thoroughly as Widow Twankey, and drew a lot of laughs.

We made enough to pay the Vancouver Hotel and be on our way back east, but individuals were virtually penniless! Tempers were getting a bit frayed too, to put it mildly. We made Edmonton, and we made Calgary and Saskatoon. People had been marvelous to us on the way. When we were due to leave Calgary, a devoted follower named Harry Yashunsky turned up at the train station with a whole hamper of food for the company. He took me on one side to apologize for the fact that the only meat he'd been able to get was ham, and if I were observant (kosher) I'd not be able to have any! Dear Harry! I lost touch, and have never known what happened to him; he would be 90, if a day, by now.

We made Regina and Winnipeg; and in Winnipeg we got stuck. We couldn't make enough money to take us on to the next place where there was a theatre big enough to house the pantomime. In Winnipeg we met again some of our friends from a few weeks earlier. We 'sang for our suppers' at Eaton's. We did anything we could think of to advertise our show, and the audiences were great! But Canadian geography beat us. The next hop (which would have been Ottawa) was too big for our purse. So the City of Winnipeg came to our rescue; we were given the Walker Theatre for two benefit performances, and for the proceeds, the CPR would take us all back to Liverpool: we had thus avoided deportation by the skin of our teeth! (see Appendix; items 4&5) I always hoped to come back to Canada in better circumstances than those in which I'd left it. Strangely, my hope was realized, twenty-one years later!

While I was in Canada Maurice Hardy had been on tour in England, with a show called *Tantivy Towers* (by A.P. Herbert and Thomas Dunhill), which required, of all things, a stage cellist! This tour collapsed at almost the same time as mine did, and we found ourselves back in London, in mid-season, with no work and very little money in the bank. Maurice lived at home with his parents and sister, and I went back to my Earl's Court room. We met almost every day, and practised without any specific goal in view, played piquet in between bouts of music, and gradually grew more and more frustrated. One day Maurice said to me, "I'd rather go and play in the streets than live like this!" "Are you serious?" said I, "if so, I'll come with you". And so the "Donkey Tour" was born. It got us publicity and concert dates, improved our health, and laid the basis for the next four years' work for us both.

≡V≡
1932: "The Donkey Tour"
(Maurice, Mélisande, and Me)

$\mathcal{T}$HE TRUCK STOPPED about a mile east of the little town of Abingdon in Berkshire. It was a cool rather damp day at the beginning of May, with the obvious promise of rain to come. Maurice and I descended from our slightly precarious positions in the body of the truck, and, with the driver's help, got our barrow down the sloping back of the truck and out into the road. The driver turned his truck, waved us good-bye, and trundled off back towards London, leaving us alone, feeling forlorn and not a little apprehensive. We were off on our big adventure; now quite committed, since we couldn't just stay where we were, in the middle of nowhere.

The barrow was a box-like contraption on two wheels, with legs at the other end so it would rest evenly on the ground when stationary. It had two handles for pushing (or pulling), and one side was considerably higher than the other. It contained a small cottage piano, and a seat which could be fitted into slots on the barrow's lower side, so that I could sit down to play. There was also floor-space for our camping and cooking equipment, clothes, other odds and ends, and for Maurice's cello. Along the top of the higher side was fixed a thick tarpaulin which could be slung over to cover all the contents of the barrow. The barrow itself was painted in gaudy black and orange stripes. It was a fine sturdy piece of work, built by a man who made barrows for the Covent Garden costers: our theory was that if one coster could push a barrow full of fruits and vegetables, the two of us could push one holding a piano. We were soon to be proved very wrong; in fact if we had known in advance what daunting struggles were ahead of us I doubt whether we should ever have embarked upon the venture of becoming itinerant musicians ("buskers"). But on that cool clammy morning our die was cast and we set about pushing our barrow into Abingdon, where we proposed to play in the streets and collect what money kind passers-by would shower into our cap. It was a somewhat battered cap, since we had kicked it around until it no longer looked new; rather it had the air of a sad old receptacle fit for the poor guys who were trying to pick up a living in the gutter.

For our first few hours we had the companionship, and the help, of a London journalist who had come down to see us started. (see Appendix, item #6) As we struggled slowly into Abingdon the rain began, and we set up our first pitch under a shop awning in the main square. I climbed up onto the piano seat; Maurice arranged himself on a camp stool at the edge of the pavement; and feeling quite desperately self-conscious, we struck up our first tune. I think it was Léhar's *You Are My Heart's Delight*. We were rewarded with a few pennies, and then the shopkeeper, obviously not a music lover, came out and pushed up his awning! The piano immediately got rained into, and before we had time to shut the top lid or to bring the tarpaulin into use, the piano's inside was dampened enough that it never really recovered. It wasn't a very good one to begin with; we'd picked it up for ten pounds in a junk-store in London!

As a source of income Abingdon was a flop; we spent a soggy afternoon. Our press reporter went back home by train, to his doubtless dry home. In the evening we fried some bacon on our primus stove and slept in a garage on a very hard concrete floor. (It was too wet to put up the tent we had brought). Nothing remains in my memory of that night but dampness, stiffness and despondency. But at least by morning the rain had stopped, our goods were dry under the tarpaulin; and after washing in a small stream, where Maurice lost his toothbrush and I trod the soap into the mud, we cooked an egg each and set out on our travels.

We had not been able to face the prospect of playing in the streets of London, where at any moment we might meet an acquaintance or a fellow-student; or even, heaven forbid, Sir Hugh Allen himself! And so the idea of the barrow and the countryside had evolved. I think that we imagined playing Beethoven and Brahms to the inhabitants of small towns and villages, and earning enough to live on, on a small scale. Our repertoire of popular music was very restricted, though we did set about enlarging it.

Maurice's father worked at the Civil Service Club and knew the people of Covent Garden, including the barrow-men, and he was a tremendous help; the parents of both of us made contributions which enabled us to have a barrow made, and to visit Scout Headquarters and other sources of camping materials. We had to be prepared to live as cheaply and simply as possible, and wear just khaki shirts and grey pants.

As we discussed where to begin, it became clear that no one place was better or worse than another, given a radius of fifty or so miles around London. We settled on Abingdon by means of a blindfold jab at a map of "London and environs"; and that is how we came to be spending so dank and disagreeable a night in an Abingdon garage, and how we came to set out next morning into the unknown, with as brave faces as we could muster. We had one definite objective at the very start; at least to get as far as Banbury, where Maurice had a pupil who had promised to arrange a recital for us as soon as we could let him know when we'd be there. We had very few pounds between us, so we set out for Witney (where the blankets are made) for we had been told that it would be market-day and the town full of people. On the way we played in a tiny village (Marsham), just to give ourselves more courage. We made only one shilling, and the school children were noisy and inquisitive!

Our progress was very slow because the barrow was heavy; the least incline seemed to increase its weight tenfold, so that either we had to use our combined full strength to budge the thing at all, or else it ran away downhill with us holding frantically onto the handles to prevent its careening into the hedge or running amok on the grass verge. However, we made Witney, only to be told by a police inspector that we needed a permit to "play in public and collect". The nearest place we could get such a permit was Oxford, so the rest of our day was taken up with a quite unnecessary bus-trip to a friendly Oxford police officer who gave us the permit, but who said "It's really not necessary at all, but that chap in Witney is very officious; I know him; good luck!" Of course when we got back to Witney the market was over; hardly anyone was around any longer; but we did play, and we made three shillings and ninepence (old

style; this was 1932!). It paid for some meat and potatoes, and we slept
that night in some hope that success might now be just around only two
or three more corners. We had our permit, we had earned a tiny bit of
money, and we were on the way to Banbury. Our next goal was Burford,
a few miles along the River Windrush, and from there it was a straight
road north to Banbury. We reached Burford; and there total disaster
appeared to overtake us.

Sixty years ago, Burford was a charming sleepy little town, with a
main street, a pretty church, old houses and cottages, and several pubs of
differing ages. It was circled by a small river, and had the air of being the
urban centre of a farming countryside, which indeed it was. It also lies
in a hollow, a fact of which we were mercifully unaware as we
approached it along the only level road entering the town, roughly following the course of the river. Our approach was very slow. It is only a
few miles from Witney to Burford, but it took us all the morning to
cover them. The barrow seemed to get heavier and heavier; to need
more and more of our strength to move it: and our muscles were trained
to make music, not to move mountains! We tried both pushing together, then one pushing while the other pulled: by half-way through the
morning we were tired out completely. Our pace had come down to
maybe one mile per hour, ten minutes' pushing and ten minutes' rest
alternately. It was a beautiful spring day but we had no eyes for the
charms of nature. All we could do was doggedly persuade our barrow
towards Burford, wondering what might transpire there; and whether,
muscle-bound as we were becoming, we should ever be able to play our
instruments again!

Around one o'clock we trudged wearily into the main street of
Burford, saw the Bear Inn a short distance up the road, and with a final
spurt of energy staggered into the courtyard, aching in every muscle.
Asking permission to park the barrow there for a while, we went into
the tap-room for beer and bread and cheese. And there, seated on two
stools at the bar, we looked at each other with a horrified query in our
eyes. We had both noticed that if we were to leave Burford along any
road except that by which we had entered, we were faced with a hill up
which we could never hope to move our barrow: we were stuck! On
only the third day out from London it seemed as though our hopes had

all foundered, and we had no idea what to do next.

There was another character sitting up at the bar; a rather disreputable and undeniably drunk old man. He had come in shortly after us and inspected us thoroughly before speaking. Then he leaned over towards us and said (and I can make no attempt at transliterating his dialect): "I see'd you fellas come into the town. What you need is a donkey. And I knows where you can get one. That'll pull the cart for you!" We laughed a little wryly at this sally; we thought he was meaning to be funny. But he was quite serious; and as we pondered his idea and commented on its possibilities, suddenly it seemed as though a donkey was what we had really needed all the time. We stood him a beer, and without thinking as yet about such minor but puzzling things as harness or shafts; or even how a donkey has to be treated; we began to get enthusiastic. It might be that we should not after all be forced to return ignominiously to London, with even less money than when we left it! The old man said, "Meet me in this here bar at six and I'll have some news for you" and he teetered amiably away.

Somehow we got through the next few hours. We arranged with the landlord of the Bear to let us sleep in his barn; there was ample room in it for us and our sleeping bags.

The barrow was in a sheltered spot and out of harm's way; and we imagined walking happily and freely along the country roads while a sturdy animal pulled our goods up hill and down dale for us. By six p.m. we were duly installed in the bar again, awaiting the old fellow whose name we didn't even know. Time passed and there was no sign of him. After waiting an hour, we asked the barman if he knew the man we'd been talking with at lunch-time, since we had a date with him and he was already an hour late. "Oh aye, I see'd 'im. That's Dick Tuck, that was; he's unreliable, as you might say. You won't ever see 'im again!"

The barman was right; we never did! But by this time we were determined to have a donkey; a donkey was the 'one thing we'd always wanted'. We explained our predicament to the barman, who was very sympathetic (as barmen are) and inclined to be helpful. "A donkey, eh? Well, let's see. I reckon there's only one man in Burford as could put you onto one, and that's young Mr. Bedford. Not the old man, but his son. Yes, young Mr. Bedford is who you ought to see."

We got directions for finding where Mr. Bedford lived ("down along by the bridge") and regardless of time of day, proper introduction, or any other proprieties, we paid for our beer and started off on our quest for Mr. Bedford and a donkey. We looked what we were, a couple of tramps, and young Mr. Bedford (young by comparison with his father, no doubt) looked at us rather sourly as we explained that we were looking for a donkey to transport our goods across the country, with Banbury the first aim. "Well now, ponies, that's another thing; or I could take you to Banbury in the truck, but donkeys? No, I dunno of any hereabouts." We were not to be put off with just one refusal, and we passed the time of evening with Mr. Bedford at his door. He seemed in no hurry to go back inside; we chatted of this and that, and took our time easy, as they do in the country.

Then, quite casually, and without gently leading back to the main reason for our visit, Mr. Bedford said "Well now, as a matter of fact I do know of a donkey. She belongs to a friend of mine who's in... well... she'm a few miles up the road; if you gents like, we could go in truck and take a look at 'er". Maurice and I, struck dumb with amazement and relief, could only nod our heads eagerly. And so, in the fading evening light, we piled into Mr. Bedford's small truck and drove a few miles up the road by which we'd entered Burford that morning. Then, stopping by a field, he said "There she be, over yon." In the semi-darkness we saw a small living form contentedly cropping grass. It had four legs, a long nose and a long tail, and we presumed it was a donkey. We tried stalking it, but we only succeeded in catching two small bushes; it'd be better by daylight. Mr. Bedford then said "Meet me at the bridge at 11 o'clock in the morning and I'll bring her over in the truck. Thirty shillings she'll cost you". It seemed too good to be true. We asked no questions about her; not age nor qualifications nor experience; and I don't think we even took in the fact that Mr. Bedford had said "she" and "her" when referring to the animal (later on we remembered all too clearly!). We didn't ask about pedigree or health; we just said, "Thanks awfully, we'll be there" and we went back to the Bear and slept like logs. It seemed we were saved, and our journey to Banbury assured.

The next morning we met our new companion. She was a charming little brown donkey. She wore a sweet and docile expression, and looked at us with big, beguiling brown eyes; and then ambled slowly across the field by the roadside and started to crop grass. So amiable an animal must surely be willing to work, and so, quite forgetting Mr. Bedford's talking of "her" and "she", we named it Barkis, who, if you remember, was "willing"[10]. That name lasted only a very short while, till we discovered that the willingness was a façade, and that at heart she was a rather stubborn melancholy little donkey, much given to tears; whether of sorrow or anger we never really found out. At any rate, after a few days we renamed her Mélisande, who was not happy either ("Je ne suis pas heureuse"). Maurice and I could never make up our minds which of us was Pelléas and which Golaud. You see, it was not so very long since the R.C.M. performance of Debussy's *Pelléas et Mélisande!*

The stipulated thirty shillings was duly paid and we now owned a donkey; and had not the faintest notion of how to set about turning her into the means of traction we needed. But clearly we now needed shafts for the barrow, and Mr. Bedford introduced us to a carpenter who came over to the Bear Inn and fixed dual shafts in place of the existing black and orange handles; all for ten shillings. Our capital was shrinking rapidly.

Then of course we needed harness; a surprising discovery for two young musicians whose only previous acquaintance with donkeys had been rides at the zoo, or at the seaside! Here again we were astonishingly lucky. The carpenter remembered that the Vicar of Burford's sister used to own a donkey when she was a girl; perhaps she still had the harness. She still lived at the vicarage, so there Maurice and I called and explained our need to a most charming elderly lady. Yes indeed, somewhere she still had that harness; and when she found it she let us have it for five shillings, complete with reins.

We were given lessons in harnessing by Mr. Bedford, who had by now quite taken to us, and after a few tries we got the hang of it. Mélisande was walked over to the Bear and we tried her between the shafts. We were enchanted with the barrow's wholly new character. By now word was getting around Burford about these two crazy young fellows with a piano and some strange stringed instrument, and a lot of camping gear and pots and pans; and young Mr. Bedford's donkey! When we finally had everything ready, maybe forty-eight hours after arriving in Burford, a minor miracle took place. We stood in front of the Bear Inn, facing north; Mélisande was properly harnessed and all our goods were neatly packed. A small crowd had gathered to watch us leave, and as we said "Tch! Tch!", and Mélisande started to walk forward, a little cheer went up from the spectators. Maurice and I were speechless, and stood for a few moments watching our barrow, this heavy, unwieldy monster which had caused us so much sweat and hard work to move. Here it was, apparently moving of its own accord, with four neat little hoofs easily seen from behind, pulling it away from us and along towards Chipping Norton and Banbury. Then we shouted good-bye to everyone, shook hands with the Bear's landlord who had charged us nothing for the use of his loft, and chased after the donkey, to shower her with praise and encouragement.

We soon found that she needed a great deal of both! She needed helping uphill, and when the barrow's weight bore on her in a downward incline she stopped altogether, and the two of us had to lean backwards against the front of the contraption, so that Mélisande imagined it wasn't there any longer and would continue her walk. Yes, she walked. We only once saw her run; and donkeys don't trot (we didn't know that either!). Her pace was two miles per hour; so that was the speed at which we walked across England. But it was twice as fast as we could manage on our own, and the muscular strain on us had been annulled, whatever mental strain our little donkey may have caused us from time to time.

A few miles out of Burford we thought we'd better see how she reacted to music, so we stopped and set up the piano seat and Maurice got out his cello, and we played to her. She took it pretty stolidly, showing no preference for one style or another. Then a fly settled on her neck, and in order to get rid of it she rubbed her neck up and down against one of the shafts, giving me, at the piano, a sort of see-saw which made it hard to find the right notes or to keep my balance! Maurice was in tucks of laughter and so was I, only Mélisande took it all quite seriously. She got rid of the fly and waited patiently for the extraordinary sounds to cease. Once, during a later performance she started to walk away with me, which was a little unnerving, but it was only a few paces, and Maurice hurried after us with his cello and his campstool and we continued playing as though nothing unusual had occurred.

We didn't know what donkeys ate, and had bought a bag of oats; a great mistake. They get too fat and lethargic on oats, and we soon stopped feeding her them, leaving her to find all the nourishment she needed by the roadside or in a field. We ourselves ate very simply; how could we do otherwise with our primitive equipment? We had a small paraffin stove, a frying pan, a pot for stew, a couple of plates and mugs and a few utensils. When "on the road", we would have bread and cheese, and maybe beer, in the middle of the day, and a warm meal in the evening. But it turned out that we were not on the road the whole time. There were periods when we stayed in someone's house, and fared a lot better than on our own cooking.

But today at any rate, we were properly "en route". We had telephoned Maurice's Banbury pupil, Mr. Cheney, that we were really on the way and we expected to arrive the following evening. We had no time schedule and were prepared to play when and where he suggested. But we warned him that we were now a "ménage à trois", and someplace would be needed for Mélisande. We sauntered along happily enough, helping the donkey when necessary, holding her safely if cars passed her too quickly (she hated cars!), and by lunchtime we'd reached Chipping Norton. Here we decided to try our luck again with our music. Mélisande behaved in exemplary fashion and people actually put money in our cap. With some misgiving we saw a policeman coming our way... were we to be "moved on" again? He merely listened gravely for a few minutes, then, saying quietly to us that "The Mayor has just given you tuppence", he put in two pennies of his own. Coppers from a cop! We made over ten shillings and were jubilant, and had a very good supper. We blessed the name of that drunken old man Dick Tuck, who probably never knew what he had done to save us; and we blessed the press, too, who had got wind of our existence and were proclaiming our impending arrival in Banbury. Henceforward we were known as "The Troubadours", and Mélisande's charming way with strangers endeared her to everyone and earned us quite a bit extra, we were certain.

While we are wandering cheerfully towards Banbury in the late afternoon, on the lookout for Mr. Cheney who was to meet us in his car and guide us to wherever he had found for us to stay; perhaps this is the time for a little more about Maurice and me. Our joining as Sonata partners at the R.C.M. had been fortuitous, but it worked well and we had played a lot together. Maurice was studying with a very fine teacher, Ivor James, and our ideas seemed to tally well. We'd given a couple of recitals, with both sonatas and solos, and our association lasted through until 1936, when Maurice went to live in the West Country and I joined the staff of the BBC. (Maurice eventually became principal cellist of the Bournemouth Symphony Orchestra). While we were working together our repertoire was of Sonatas by Beethoven, Brahms, Debussy, Kodaly, Bach and Mendelssohn. Later we added Fauré. And there were solo items by many composers. For us to attempt a "popular" repertoire for busking out of doors was quite an undertaking, and any offer for us to play more serious music would be eagerly accepted.

I stood only five foot three. Maurice was a good head taller than I, and was already losing his hair, which made him look older than he really was. He was very patient with Mélisande until the slow pace would become intolerably irksome for him, and he would stride ahead for a mile or so; only to turn around and come back to meet us, still trundling along at two m.p.h.! We were an oddly assorted pair in some ways, perhaps, but musically in sympathy, and sharing a sense of humour which made our donkey-tour as possible for us as was our playing. We played well in those days! And we were determined to play our sonatas from memory too. This slightly curtailed our repertoire, but it did add some spontaneity to the performances!

So much for our history. At present, we were at one and the same time friends, musicians, and Mélisande's slaves. And as such we were eventually greeted by Mr. Cheney, a mile or so outside Banbury. It was for us a momentous meeting; the arrangements he had made radically altered the form of our work on this journey. We were to stay in the garden of the organist of the parish church, and there was a field for the donkey. We were to give a recital in a very charming old concert room; and we were also scheduled to play at two or three schools in the area. These school concerts, done for a nominal fee, were to become the mainstay of our tour. For people living as we did, a fee of two or three guineas represented riches beyond anything we'd dreamed of.

We were received most kindly by the organist, Mr. Palmer, and his wife. We put up our tent in their garden and settled Mélisande in her field, safely tied to a tree by a long rope supplied by Mr. Palmer. And then we were invited to supper in the house; a real treat after our few days of roughing it. A day or so later, when the spring rain started again, Mrs. Palmer was so disturbed by the idea of how wet we might get in our tent, that she prepared a spare bedroom for us, and we found ourselves once again sleeping in proper beds. It seemed a little too soft for "tramps", but it was certainly very comfortable.

Altogether Banbury remains a very pleasant memory; the recital went well, and so did the school concerts. We played our serious repertoire, and never did we find it necessary to play down to young audiences: that is an unforgiveable attitude! They would take the best we could offer, and we enjoyed playing for them. One school caused us some misgivings.

It was a small and very select public (private!) school for boys, where sport was the most important thing, and the arts hardly got any attention. Perhaps it was the novelty of two musical tramps plus donkey which persuaded the headmaster to invite us. He was quite clearly as nervous as we were of the outcome! But after the concert (an hour in length) he pronounced it "Splendid! As good as a half-holiday!" and we felt we had made the grade. The Head phoned to a school in Stratford-on-Avon on our behalf, thus securing us another engagement.

One afternoon, as we were sitting in Mr. Cheney's office finalizing arrangements for our concert room recital, a phone call came through from the police. A donkey was wandering loose in the town, and they had reason to believe that Mr. Cheney knew the owners. Could he please have them come and recapture their pet? We fled as fast as we could, looking around for Mélisande, and eventually found her contentedly admiring Banbury Cross! (Yes, there really is one, right at the town's centre). Maurice rode her back to the field (for Mélisande that was the depth of ignominy!) and we found a stouter rope to secure her to the tree. Her escapade soon became known, and people seemed to be more eager to see her than to hear us!

We must have spent a full week in Banbury, and it was with real regret that we said thank you and good-bye to the Palmers and Mr. Cheney, and set out once more with our barrow. We headed in the direction of Stratford-on-Avon, where we had school concerts already arranged. The headmasters and headmistresses of the schools we'd played at passed on word of our coming; and so, although we and Mélisande travelled as slowly as ever, we hardly ever again played in the streets, and the little cottage piano got more and more out of tune, from lack of use.

When we had left Burford, complete with donkey and all her accessories, we had hardly any money at all, maybe just under a pound between us. I guess we could have phoned our parents for help, but we had no wish to acknowledge such a degree of defeat so early in the game. After our week in Banbury we were rich; several pounds in our pockets and the promise of more to come! Schools were not wealthy enough to provide fees on a "city scale", but we were not asking for such recognition. After all, we were tramps! But, our new wealth buoyed us up, and even the damp cold morning on which we left Banbury was tolerable enough to keep us in reasonable spirits. Mélisande behaved well and we made good time. The press had been kind to us in Banbury, and people were on the lookout for us: all in all we felt that our venture would, even after so unpropitious a start, prove in the end to be worthwhile.

As the day wore on the weather got worse, and we decided to use some of our Banbury earnings to take a room in a pub at a village along the road, and so avoid what was obviously going to be a wet, cold night. Around five p.m. Maurice strode on ahead to find lodgings for the night, and he promised to come back and meet us later. Mélisande and I trudged on while the rain came down in earnest, and the hours seemed very long indeed. In the gathering dusk Maurice finally appeared out of the gloom, bringing welcome news of a room reserved at a little hotel in Wellesbourne Hastings, a village now only some two miles away. He had also arranged for six bottles of beer to be put on one side, in case we should arrive after closing time. We were all wet, and this prospect served to cheer us up, except for Mélisande. She now took charge of the proceedings. She stopped, planted her forelegs wide apart and stood stock still while glaring at us with undisguised malice. Quite clearly she was not going to budge another inch in such weather!

We didn't yet know much about donkeys! We didn't know, for instance, that their hides are very thick and that one good swipe on her rear end with the reins would probably have made her understand that she was required to continue walking. No. We were "kind to animals" and this poor little bedraggled moke was our responsibility. We pushed at her, and pulled at her; but all to no avail. There seemed no alternative but to stay right where we were, in the middle of nowhere. A wide grass verge at the side of the road allowed room for the tent; a high hedge afforded a little shelter from the wind; and so we unharnessed Mélisande and tied her to a convenient gate. In a very bad temper we pitched our small tent, managing not to get the inside wet, and then set about frying sausages in the rain. We did keep the stove alight, but the sausages spat, and we had no potatoes. It was a horrid supper on a beastly night. Enticing visions of a dry pub and bubbling tankards of beer floated before our minds' eyes and made us even more out of spirits. Mélisande seemed quite content (damn her!), now that she was out of harness, and for us that was the last straw. In almost complete darkness we crept into our sleeping-bags, clothes, boots and all; and waited for a little warmth to seep into our bodies and send us to sleep.

As I began at last to feel a bit of warmth and comfort, we heard the quiet sound of a bicycle splashing along the deserted road. It stopped right by our tent, heavy footsteps approached us, and a torch was shone through the tent-flap. Our nervousness was transformed into sheer rage as we discerned, behind the torch, the form of a large policeman in a glittering wet shoulder cape. "Now then" said the policeman, "what are you doing here?" It seemed a particularly silly question, and I, who was nearer the tent's exit, answered; with no thought at all about the majesty of the law, or of being polite to strangers: "We're camping by the side of the road, that's what we're doing". "Well, you can't do that there in Warwickshire, that you can't" replied the bobby; "Who are you any-way?" We told him, in terse and vigorous language, who we were and why we were there. So what? If we spent the night in clink it would at least be dry. But to our surprise the policeman was completely mollified! "Oh" said he, "I thought you was gypsies. Far too many of them around for my liking. But God forbid I should prevent anyone from trying to earn a living these days". Now totally friendly, the policeman bade us goodnight and good luck, and cycled off into the rain; doubtless to some cozy, dry cottage, with a hot supper awaiting him. As for us, we started all over again to try and get warm; and Mélisande said nothing.

The early morning sun awakened us; warm and shining through the tent; bringing comfort and a certain stuffiness! We crawled out, messy and unkempt, to see a perfectly cloudless sky; no sign of last night's downpour except the dampness of the grass, which very soon evaporated. In this gorgeous brightness the whole of last night's discomfort and disappointment seemed even more pointless. And there was Mélisande, all bright-eyed innocence, saying, "Good morning, chaps! Isn't it a beautiful day?" We cursed her vehemently, and then set about spreading out our things to dry in the sun. The bacon sizzled appetizingly and we enjoyed our breakfast. The only casualty of the night was one of Maurice's bows, which came unglued because of the abrupt change in temperature. This repair would have to wait until we got to Bristol, where Mr. Maby, the cello expert, lived.

We assembled ourselves in leisurely fashion, enjoying the sunshine and the really beautiful country view of trees, fields, low hills and a few farms. Then, with the donkey again between the shafts, we started out towards Stratford. We approached the pub where we should have spent the night; just then Mélisande gave us an exhibition which she never again repeated. She took one sideways look at the pub, and broke into a *run*. She ran right through the village (Wellesbourne Hastings). Our pots and pans clanged and jangled and fell off their hooks; we pelted after the barrow, picking things up as they clattered into the road; both of us quite astonished at Mélisande's strength, and at her conscience! As soon as the last house in the village was passed, she resumed her two-mile-an-hour amble. She made no comment, nor did we ever see her run with the barrow again. The whole thing was inexplicable. The rest of the day proceeded in its customary dignified manner; no hurry, no more caprices, just two miles an hour; but for days afterwards we would burst into laughter at the mere memory of that chase!

"Wellesbourne Hastings" may seem a very grandiose name for what was only a small village, but in that part of England such double-barreled names are quite common. They usually denote the marriage (centuries ago) between two families whose names have become perpetuated by the villages which grew up around the manor house. Worcestershire is particularly rich in such place-names, and we derived a lot of pleasure from them. Our favourites were Flyford Flavell, Upton Snodsbury, and

Martin Hussingtree. And then, also in Worcestershire, there is Wyre Piddle. There are a number of "Piddles" in Dorset. In Victorian times, some effort was made to get rid of this rather vulgar word; though not always successfully. The River Piddle was renamed, most unimaginatively, the Trent; but on its banks there was still the little town of Piddletrenthyde! Then there were the "Puddles" which must have seemed more decorous (Tolpuddle, Affpuddle, Turner's Puddle, Puddletown...) but it appeared to us just as much of a pity to obscure ancient history by changing these names as it is to hide the origins of the English language by phonetic spelling reforms. I have never been able to understand how so eloquent a writer as George Bernard Shaw could have lent his name to a movement which could only result in English hiding its various derivations under a cloak of phonetic anonymity. (Maybe because he was Irish?)

Be that as it may, these double-barreled names intrigued us very much, as did the dialects we met as we travelled westwards. We moved from Oxfordshire, through Warwick, Worcester, Gloucester, into Somerset and Dorset. Everywhere we went, as tramps, we frequented the taprooms of pubs rather than the "Saloon Bars" where the gentry did their drinking. The one thing to be done in a pub in any western county is to play "shove-halfpenny" or else "table skittles"; both of them excellent games and good substitutes for darts. (By the way, the first one is pronounced shuv-hayp'ny). The chaps in the taprooms were all farmhands or labourers, and though they were most friendly with us two "foreign" tramps, we found them hard to understand. It is amazing how, in so small a country as England (no place is more than 100 miles from the sea) the dialects are so various and so different! Not that we spent all our spare time drinking in pubs, but the English country pub used, in those days, to be a very effective club which provided companionship, conversation and gentle amusement of an evening.

At some point on our way we had to have proper shoes made for Mélisande; the high roads were hard on her own hoofs and I think she was grateful for the relief. It was at a real old-fashioned smithy that we had it done, while we waited. I think this was the occasion when we met "Chacewater Charlie". Charlie was, like us, "on the road", and he viewed us with some considerable misgiving. Indeed, his eye could well have been called jaundiced, until he realized that we were buskers, and he wasn't, so he could afford to be friendly. He was a jaunty little man, very pleased with himself, and he told us how successful he was. "I'm clever, I am; but then so are you, I'll bet. We're all clever!" We looked out for Chacewater Charlie as we got nearer the sea, but we didn't meet him again. We did meet, though, one of the most contented men I have ever known. He was a real tramp. That is, he spent all the spring, summer and earlier autumn months walking around the countryside. He had no special goals; any odd job which might turn up, he would do. Once a month he went to a post office, wherever he happened to be, and drew the small pension on which he lived. He slept rough; out of doors: and he and I walked for many miles one day while Maurice was on one of his brisk walks ahead. When he rejoined us, we three continued on until evening. I can no longer remember what we talked about, but conversation never flagged all day long. When Maurice and I decided we'd gone far enough, and found a pleasant field in which to camp, we offered to share our supper with the tramp (we never did learn his name) and his company overnight, though our tent only held two. But he refused, very courteously, saying, "No, two's company and three's none. I'll be on my way a little further" and he walked on into the evening. He seemed to have no ambition any longer; no grouches, no regrets. His philosophy was simple and positive, and he was happy. Only the winter, which he had to spend in cheap lodging-houses, caused him displeasure. His simplicity was both wise and charming, and he made a great impression on us.

Now I may have intimated that of the two of us, Maurice was the more impatient, but this was not so. His walks ahead were less frequent than mine, and he kept his patience with Mélisande longer than I did: perhaps the cello is a more philosophically inclined instrument than is a piano! But it is true that at two miles an hour one can almost count the blades of grass along the roadside, and the small hedgerow flowers are seen to be bright gems amid all the green surroundings. Cars and trucks seem to be wild, turbulent intruders into the quietness of the country. Mélisande certainly did not like them and was apt to shy if one passed her too fast or too noisily, especially coming up from behind. On the whole, she was inclined to ignore other animals, though there were two horses in Stratford in whom she showed unusual interest; and once we passed a field with another donkey in it. Mélisande's behaviour was distinctly coy! She was certainly aware of the other donkey, and pulled over to the other side of the road to get close enough to so they could rub noses.

But generally, donkeys were a rarity; maybe most of them were congregated at seaside resorts giving rides to small children. Only in Dorset did farmers still keep a donkey amongst the cattle, "to catch the diseases", it was said. Sheep, Mélisande studiously ignored, if she met any! She paid as little attention to them as she did to the music which, in the first few days of our joint lives, she heard from Maurice and me. Of course, she never had to listen to us playing tunes which lasted more than two or three minutes. Our practising of Beethoven, Debussy and other more serious music was done as and when we found opportunity. Already in Burford we were told of a gentleman who owned a grand piano, and we had persuaded him to let us use it for a couple of hours. And in Banbury, of course, Mr. Palmer's music-room was at our disposal when he was not teaching; which didn't seem to be too frequent during the few days we spent there. As our journeying became increasingly simply a means of covering the distances between the schools to which we had invitations to play, practising became less of a problem. And those school concerts were not only rewarding in themselves; they turned out to be the foundation of our next three or four years' work!

So, our fortune was set in Banbury: and I have left us pelting through Wellesbourne Hastings on our way to Stratford, where we had introductions to two or three schools, including the ancient Grammar School which William Shakespeare had once attended!

We duly reached Stratford and presented ourselves at the school which we thought might be able to help us find a place to camp, and to accommodate Mélisande. Our arrival coincided with a school break, and the boys came trooping out to see our donkey and the contraption it pulled. To our surprise and pleasure, we were given the use of a wooden pavilion at the far end of their cricket field, with the whole field available to the donkey! True, it was also inhabited by two horses, but she and they soon made great friends; Mélisande seemed to admire them unreservedly and ambled around happily after them. When we eventually left Stratford, Mélisande was clearly very sad, and the horses came to the fence to watch our departure. But, a lot happened between our arrival and departure. We had schools to play at, and at each school we received our fee in cash. Cheques would have been no use to us anyway.

We wandered around Stratford, admiring the lovely old houses, and also the Memorial Theatre, then comparatively new and beautiful in its surroundings of trees, green lawns and the River Avon, complete with swans. Our cricket pavilion was cozy; wooden floors were by then no hardship to us; and one evening we sat at the little table and counted our earnings. They made a goodly sight; some banknotes, and lots of silver and copper, which we would take to the post office and convert into paper money. We were well satisfied with our finances, stowed the money away, and after a quiet game of piquet (our cards were black and orange-backed like the barrow, too!) we settled down for the night. I slept on my tummy; Maurice slept on his back; and suddenly he began to laugh. Without turning over to look, I asked him why. But he could give no other response than more laughter. Finally, I sat up and rather indignantly demanded to know what it was all about. And then I saw, and burst out laughing too. For outside, silhouetted against the window, was the top half of a very large policeman. Another cop! We got up and opened the door to him. "I saw a light in the pavilion" said he, "and I thought midnight seems a mighty odd time to have a light on in a cricket pavilion, so I came over to see. And who might you be, and what might you be doing?" He seemed quite satisfied with our explanation of ourselves, told us all about his young son who played some brass instrument or other, and took himself off into the night. We were very relieved indeed that he had not visited us earlier and found us surrounded by all that money. It would, we felt, have looked rather suspicious. After all, we didn't any longer look much like young gentlemen, our complexions having by now been hardened and darkened by wind, rain and sun. A couple of young Bill Sykes would have been nearer the mark!

Next morning, having no special plans, we were sitting outside in the sun, doing nothing in particular, when we received another visitor. The tall handsome man introduced himself as Wilfred Walter, the actor, then appearing at the Memorial Theatre. We knew his name very well indeed, and he had heard of us from Helen Henschel. Mr. Walter had enquired from one pub to another for us, knowing we were in Stratford. (Yes, we did keep a little in touch with the outside world.) Then, at last, he caught sight of our barrow and came over to see us. He was staying with friends in the country, not too far from Stratford, and he brought us an invitation to come and spend Sunday with them; they would pick us up in their car. This was a great surprise to us, and a very pleasant one too; and as it turned out, was the beginning of a long friendship with Wilfred Walter's friends, the Gibbons.

They lived in an old and quite charming house, Abberton Hall, at the centre of a very small village. There were a few cottages, a little steepled church which one could see from miles around, and a great expanse of farming and grazing country. The Gibbons' house itself, gracious in its simplicity, faced a beautifully kept garden, looked after by Mrs. Gibbon. It was full of masses of blue and mauve aubretia; a low wall bounded the nearer part of the garden, and the view southwards was of lush fields, big trees, and a vast sweep of sky. Breathtaking. One could take in all the beauty of the panorama, sitting on the flagged terrace outside the front of the house, which is where we had our drinks before lunch.

It had been quite bewildering to reach this place so quickly, after our accustomed donkey-pace! We met the whole family; Captain Gibbon, a short spare man in his fifties; his wife, a charming lady (no taller than her husband), who looked the epitome of the English country gentlewoman, with her wide straw hat and gardening gloves and clippers never far away! They had two sons, Mike and Ben, who were a few years younger than Maurice and me. I think the Estate must have been fairly extensive; I never learnt exactly how large an acreage it was, but Captain Gibbon spent much of his time overseeing its upkeep. Those were still the days of staff and servants; the house and land were very carefully looked after.

The Gibbons were interested in all the arts. The boys both drew and painted well, and also seemed to be able to make music on a large variety of wind instruments; there was a room full of them! Flute, oboe, clarinet, even a bass clarinet; horn, trumpet and a tuba. They had a good piano, too, and a collection of gramophone records. There were flowers everywhere in the house, and we learnt that customarily, even if they were alone, the Gibbon family "dressed for dinner" in the evenings;

drinks at 6, dinner at 7, allowing time to change in between. Of course, Maurice and I had little to change into, but I think that Sundays were exceptions.

Mrs. Gibbon's unmarried sister (name of Chafy) lived just behind Abberton Hall, in a picturesque thatched cottage. Two old labourers' houses had been knocked into one, and the whole thing renovated in appropriate taste; old wooden furniture with gracious lines, and again, flowers everywhere. The two sisters were much of an age, and were very conscious indeed that their family had lived in that particular bit of Worcestershire "since before the Conquest". As the Conquest was that of William I of Normandy, 1066 A.D. that meant close on a thousand years!

The Gibbons and Miss Chafy were delightful and cultivated people, interesting and interested, and they gave Maurice and me a halcyon day. Indeed, the only disagreeable member of the household was a rather bad-tempered parrot who would pay no attention to anybody but Captain Gibbon himself. It was sometimes taken from its cage and put into a tree, where it sat glaring angrily at any human beings who happened to be around. If it flopped down from the tree, it was to waddle fiercely after some lady croquet-player and try to bite her ankles. Captain Gibbon had to be hurriedly summoned to effect a rescue! He had, he said, spent years trying to teach the bird to say "One, two, three, four, six... dammit I've forgotten five!" Quite useless. The bird never got further than "One", which it used to emit in a raucous squawk. It was, however, the only member of the household with whom I felt little in common!

Our day at Abberton Hall passed all too quickly, but before we were driven back to our cricket field, we were invited to bring Mélisande and come back to spend a few days with the Gibbon family. We could practise to our hearts' content; play to them in the evenings if we felt like it; and they would be able to provide us with introductions in Worcester and its surroundings. Since our general route was to take in the city of Worcester, and since the day had been so lovely, we accepted out of hand. We would leave Stratford and walk slowly along the country roads till we got to Abberton; and surely, we would play everything we knew for the Gibbons if they wanted to hear it! Mélisande would have a few more days rest; we were most touched by such great friendliness, and were very grateful.

All our engagements back in Stratford fulfilled, and armed with an introduction to the headmaster of Evesham Grammar School (should we go that way), we packed up, harnessed a reluctant Mélisande, and left the same day, those two horses watching us over the fence till we were out of sight. Like the River Avon itself, we moved out of Warwickshire into Worcestershire, leaving the Cotswold Hills behind and heading forward to where, far ahead, the Malverns beckoned us. We were approaching the West Country proper; and with a few days' holiday into the bargain.

I can remember little about the walk to Abberton. I have a fancy that it took place at night and that Mélisande objected strongly. I can also remember the sight of a mill, by a large stream, with all its windows glowing; either lighted from within or else reflecting the rising sun. The mental picture is so vivid that it must have been a reality. The only explanation can be that indeed we did leave Stratford at night; no wonder Mélisande demurred!

We were made very welcome by the Gibbons; the barrow was parked in a barn, and Mélisande was turned out to grass in a wild part of the grounds. Maurice and I were each given a room and were able to unpack all our belongings to take stock of what tidying and washing was needed. The house was so old that there was only one room upstairs which had running water, so every morning we'd find a jug of hot water placed outside our rooms, for washing and shaving. We thoroughly enjoyed our few days' holiday; a respite from being tramps and a rest from helping Mélisande drag our worldly goods from place to place. Our hosts were great company, and in addition to their treating us like kings at home, they drove us all around the countryside to see the little Worcestershire villages; including one which possessed a great rarity; a sixteenth century church with a black-and-white wooden tower, gable-roofed in the old Tudor style.

They also helped us to find school dates in Worcester and Malvern, so that when we left we had a number of introductions, and moreover, a place to stay when we reached Worcester. First, though, we planned to visit Evesham, where we had a probable date at the Grammar School. It was with real reluctance that we packed up the barrow once again, said 'au revoir' to the Gibbons and set out southwards for Evesham. The town's only interest for musicians (unless you're going to play there) is that Muzio Clementi spent the last years of his life there, and is buried in the parish church's cemetery.

I can't remember any longer where we camped in Evesham, but I know that we found Mélisande a nice green patch by a gas station, and tied her to a post by her long rope. We thought she would have ample room to walk about, eat, lie down, and generally be at ease. Alas, in the morning when we visited her, we found a lamentable sight. She had walked round and round the post, always in the same direction. She had churned the grass up into a mess of mud, and was standing with her forehead jammed against the post, unable to think what to do next! She seemed to be weeping real tears, and into the bargain the flies were bothering her. Poor Mélisande; surely now she could truthfully say "Je ne suis pas heureuse". We unwound her and petted her until she was a little comforted. Then we borrowed a hose from the gas station and washed her down; whereat, so happy to be free and clean again was she, that she promptly lay down and rolled around in the dust, of which we had just finished ridding her! We came near to losing our tempers with her, but went to look for a better spot to tether her.

That day, too, we presented our credentials to the headmaster of Evesham Grammar School, Mr. Hazelhurst. He had indeed heard of us from his friend in Stratford, but he was taking no chances, and subjected us to "Ordeal by Music". He had his young son play to us on the cornet (O Star of Eve!); neither of us batted an eyelid and both of us said how talented the boy was! I suppose that got us our date, but I do not recall its having been a particularly successful one, since the boys were restless and clearly unused to music (unless maybe the cornet!).

We played at all sorts of schools during our time on the road. In those days English schools were either for girls or for boys; co-educational schools were a rarity except for the younger grades at Elementary Schools. There were the Public Schools (In North America they're called Private!) and the Grammar Schools for boys, High Schools for girls, and smaller preparatory schools for either sex. We didn't have the chance to play at any of the big Public Schools until later in our career, nor yet at any of the few co-educational boarding schools run by the Quakers. But we managed plenty of variety just the same.

Our programmes were usually of a set pattern: we would open with a Sonata for both of us (maybe an eighteenth century one with a sort of Continuo keyboard part), then each of us played a group of solos. Our final item was the same everywhere; a *Bolero for Cello Solo* with piano accompaniment, by Rubio. In the second half of this piece, the cellist discards his bow and plays a lively Spanish dance, all pizzicato (strings plucked with the fingers). Maurice played this with great style, and with many sinuous twistings of his right arm; he treated his cello as though it were a guitar. This always brought the house down, and usually also caused much giggling and sometimes outright laughter. There was one girls' school however, where, on a return visit, Maurice was asked to omit that piece from his programme! It had clearly proved too much for the headmistress, or somebody! Too suggestive, perhaps?

One school stands out in my memory; a small Quaker prep school for boys in the Malverns, where the headmaster, Geoffrey Hoyland, was a music enthusiast. The highest compliment he could pay one of his boys was to invite him to join the choir which sang Bach; and on Sunday evenings he would have a gramophone concert in his study, which any boy might attend if he wished; the only stipulation was "no talking". That audience took all we had to offer; Debussy, Kodaly, as well as Beethoven, Brahms, Chopin and Mendelssohn. In addition, we were made free of a lovely outdoor swimming pool, which was great in the summer heat. The school also boasted a model railway (lifesize and functional) which previous generations of boys had helped make. Real trains ran on certain days and at weekends, driven by senior boys, and the track was attended to by juniors. That headmaster was an exceptional man. I knew one of the boys who went through his hands; he became a most civilized and well-informed person himself, and a successful citizen and human being. I kept in touch with Mr. Hoyland for a long time after that first concert at his school.

Usually we were paid in cash, given us by one of the staff at the end of the concert; it might amount to one, two, or even three pounds. But at one small girls' school, when the applause was over, we observed a child solemnly passing along the rows of chairs with a big wooden plate, into which each member of the audience put her own contribution.

Sensing what was likely to happen, Maurice made a dive for his cello case and spent an inordinately long time packing his instrument away, inspecting every inch of it as he did so, surrounded by a group of admiring little girls. I was left standing, after having arranged and rearranged our music on the side of the piano as often as I could! But there was no escape. Maurice was still busy, and so the girl with the collecting plate approached me, and tipped into my cupped hands a pile of pennies, threepenny bits and sixpences, which with great difficulty I managed to transfer to my trouser pockets: about thirty shillings in all! I had to keep my hands in my pockets for the rest of the afternoon, to prevent embarrassing disaster!

(A "threepenny bit" pronounced thrip'ny, was the smallest silver coin produced by the Royal Mint. It was thin, and tiny, and easily lost, and not long after this it was discontinued. The only place where you would constantly be given these irritating little coins was in Scotland; where it was obligatory to put silver into the collection plate in church, but never too much!)

Mostly the proceedings were very informal at these school concerts; indeed I remember one school for infants where we had four and five year olds sprawling on the floor at our feet as we played. But, in contrast, there was an extremely "high-class" and sober school in Malvern where the girls, all dressed in grey, trooped in in single file and stood to attention in front of their chairs until given permission to sit down. Their reception of our music was as restrained as their behaviour, and we found we could not play very well for them.

At many places we made real friends, and returned during the ensuing years to play more formally; and a little more normally attired for a concert, too. (This was long, long before the days when it became "de rigueur" to go onto the platform in a turtleneck and jeans!) But, on the Donkey Tour we knew that the non-appearance of Mélisande on the platform was a real disappointment! She wasn't even always with us, for, with our base in Worcester for two weeks, we visited schools in that area by train or bus, while Mélisande stayed in an apple orchard at Mr. Powell's farm at Upper Wick.

School folk were very kind to us everywhere, made us welcome, sometimes fed us, and sometimes found us places to pitch our tent. In

Somerset one headmistress put a disused grass tennis court at our disposal, and told us that between 8:00 and 8:30 a.m., while the girls were
at breakfast, we might use the bathroom for washing and shaving. "I'll
show you which room" she said, and threw open the door. Inside was all
steamy, with a girl taking a tub. Miss Aldwinkle said "*Oh!*" and shut the
door hastily. We of course never knew which of our subsequent audience had been so rudely disturbed! Nevertheless, it was true that
between 8:00 and 8:30 in the mornings the house seemed deserted, and
Maurice and I were hardly ever so clean and well-groomed on the road,
as during those few days.

School pianos were a source of much tribulation; they might be sharp
or flat or just generally indeterminate; and in each case Maurice had to
do some impromptu adjusting in his playing. At one school the piano
was so awful that after the first movement of our opening item, I gave
up completely, and said that I could not continue that Sonata on this
instrument! Whereupon the mistress in charge said "Oh well, you'd better use our *good* piano, then" and we all trooped into another room
where a quite reasonable grand piano made the concert possible. Perhaps
she had felt that tramps didn't deserve grand pianos. But the worst of all
was in a farmhouse, where the piano was a minor third flat! (But that
belongs in the next part of our story).

While Mélisande lived in Mr. Powell's apple orchard, we lived in his
dry and comfortable barn. With that as our "pied-à-terre" we visited in
Worcester, Malvern and district, and I remember with particular pleasure
the King's School, just by Worcester Cathedral, where our audience of
boys was more attentive and receptive than many an adult audience.
Only, we had to wait quite a long time while the great Cathedral clock
chimed the hour; it was too loud to play through! The headmaster, Dr.
Creighton, was a most courteous and civilized gentleman (surely a relative of the famous Bishop of Worcester of the same name); he made us
welcome as human beings as well as itinerant musicians. We conversed
contentedly with him, whilst watching him pursue his hobby of petit-
point; he had handstitched all his chair seats and chair backs himself.

The two weeks spent at the Powell farm were, professionally, the peak
of our tour. (One afternoon each week there was a folk-dancing practise on Mr. Powell's lawn: we rather rudely called one of their dances

"making porridge") This time was also the summit of Mélisande's bliss. And of course, she ate too much! When we came to saddle and harness her, prior to moving on, she would barely fit between the shafts! Mr. Powell said, "My! She's fat. She almost looks like she might be with foal!" Most unfortunately Mélisande heard him, and more unfortunately still, she apparently understood English; this all led to the most alarming of all our adventures.

Our route now lay southwards, for we were bound for Taunton, in Somerset, and had to pass through Tewkesbury, Gloucester, and Bristol. But we had not long left Worcester behind, when Mélisande began to behave very strangely. She would go along quite happily for awhile, and then suddenly would start weaving about from side to side of the road, to the danger of any oncoming traffic, and of ourselves. Then she would stop, sigh dejectedly, weep a few tears, and plod on. We negotiated Tewkesbury, where, in a café we met an ex-R.C.M. student whom we both knew. I think he was now the organist of Tewkesbury; certainly he was always immaculately dressed. He was obviously acutely embarrassed to be greeted publicly by a couple of very disreputable-looking tramps. We made the most of his unease (very unsporting of us!), talked very loudly and slapped him on the back; and then went on our way chortling rather unkindly. Poor Freddie!

We made Gloucester, Mélisande becoming more and more erratic and temperamental. Remembering Mr. Powell's parting remarks about foals made us terribly anxious about our lady companion; for of her womanly status we were now altogether convinced. Not far from Bristol, she was down to about one mile an hour, halting and weaving and balking; and around noon we stopped for bread and cheese and beer at a small country pub. There, in the bar, were a number of men, all obviously 'off the land'; after a suitable period for desultory conversation, we summoned up our courage and asked if anyone there knew anything about donkeys, for we thought ours was in foal and we were worried stiff. One old fellow said, "Oh, aye. I knows all about donkeys; I were brought up wi'em" and out he came to inspect Mélisande.

He eyed her from every angle, prodded her in one or two uncomfortable places, whereat she kicked him, and then he pronounced, "Aye, she'm in foal all right". We blenched: "When might it happen?" "Most any time now" said the expert. "And what does one do?...I mean, how long...? How will she...?" we stuttered. "Oh, as to that, it'll be weaned a' six-month". We had the most appalling visions of our future progress, complete with baby. Hoping against hope that he was wrong, we thanked our medical adviser, and encouraged Mélisande to go on a little further. And only a little further would she go! I'm sure she had been quite aware of what was taking place, and after another hundred yards or thereabouts, she stopped dead in her tracks, turned her mournful eyes on us and said "Boys; it's going to happen any minute now. For heaven's sake get me into a field or something". We were right opposite a farmhouse with acres of fields stretching behind and around it; good fortune thus far! We tied her to a gate and went up to the house. The farmer's wife was at home, and we explained our - or rather, Mélisande's - predicament. Could we *please* borrow a bit of one of their fields while the birth took place? The farmer's wife was most understanding and sympathetic. Inside ten minutes, Mélisande, the barrow, and we were in a fine big field maybe a couple of hundred yards behind the farm buildings. We unharnessed the donkey, who staggered to the farthest corner of the field and sank down exhausted on the ground. *We* went in search of a public telephone, and called the RSPCA in Bristol: "For pete's sake send out a veterinary accoucheur to Mr. X's farm in Falfield; we don't know what to do!" The man at the other end said no one could come for two or three days, but he took the address and promised that we should be visited within a short time. That was a bit reassuring, but in three days anything might happen, and probably would! Mélisande took no notice of us, she just stayed alone in her corner, getting up occasionally to nibble a bit of grass, and then collapsing again in misery.

Meanwhile we put up our tent, bought a few provisions at the farm, and tried to get used to the idea of becoming a quartet. In the evening, when the farmer had come home and heard the story, he insisted we should pay them a visit a little later on, have a drink, and "give us a bit of music". Well, a "bit of music" was the least repayment we could offer for such unquestioning friendliness, but alas! When we had had our drink and came into the parlour, where the piano was; I gave Maurice an "A" to tune to, and it sounded "F sharp"! The entire instrument was a minor third flat! Maurice firmly refused to transpose, so it was I who played all the popular songs and folk-tunes in an old album a minor third *up*, while Maurice peered from a distance and played what he was able to see. Mr. and Mrs. "Farmer" were delighted with this entertainment, and we went off to our tent feeling that we had earned our keep; and praying that Mélisande would survive the night.

Seeing that we had to wait for two or three days for the vet to visit us, and that neither of us could do a thing to help Mélisande, we took a bus into Bristol. Maurice took his cello and went to see Mr. Maby whose shop was a sort of Mecca for cellists; he had a great reputation as an expert in all things pertaining to cellos, and Maurice's, after so much jolting on the barrow and so much exposure to different weather conditions, could well do with inspection, if nothing more. Also there was the bow to be mended. I, promising Maurice a good supper, went off to find Fortt's (the Fortnum & Mason of Bristol) and there bought us a meal of the most delectable delicatessen I could find in their store. We met up again at the bus station, and later that evening had what was to us an Epicurean meal of stupendous proportions. And Mélisande stayed in her corner and moped... no sign of a foal.

Well, the RSPCA man finally arrived, looked her over, and told us she was no more with foal than we were! She was too fat and had obviously eaten too much. She needed exercise, and after a day's *running* around she should be quite able to do her work. So, Mélisande was ridden all over the farm by the farmer's children. She hated every second of it, poor darling! It hurt her dignity to be ridden by a human being, adult or child; it caused her a lot of what she felt was unnecessary exertion, and was altogether a great humiliation. But she did lose a lot of weight! The farmer's kids had a marvelous day, and so did we. We were so relieved, and also rather angry with the poor beast; though to be sure, we had had no idea that our every word was being understood. But clearly, she knew the game was up!

With Maurice's cello in good repair, the spirits of both of us uplifted again, we harnessed the moke once more; and this time she made no demur. We said thank you and good-bye to the farmer, his wife and family, and pushed on again towards Bristol. Curiously, as though to make some atonement, Mélisande did sixteen miles that day; right through Bristol and out the other side, without any complaints at all!

We were making for Taunton, by way of Weston-super-Mare. We had discovered that if Mélisande was being extra dilatory, a whack on her rear with the end of the reins produced a slightly increased speed. It looked a bit cruel perhaps, but her hide was very thick, and I think the whack tickled rather than hurt. Of course, we ought to have found that out much earlier on, but we were soft-hearted about Mélisande! On our way into Weston she was being very irritating again, and our use of the reins from time to time must have been observed by someone who promptly reported us to the RSPCA. Presently a small car pulled up near us, and an Inspector came over to see what was going on. He found no evidence of mistreatment; only a sore being rubbed up by her collar. We were aware of this, but hadn't yet thought of any way of dealing with it. (A bit stupid, eh?) The inspector advised us to get some ointment and a different type of collar, and told us where in Weston we could buy them. Mélisande was far more comfortable with her new collar, and the sore disappeared in a few days.

Still, we plodded on towards Taunton. We had a date there, at Taunton School, whose headmaster, Mr. Nicholson, hailed, as I did, from Manchester. And we also had an invitation to rest up for a few days, at the home of an acquaintance of my father's. She was a lady of later middle age, living with a companion (whom she bossed around a good deal, to our embarrassment) in a big house some six miles outside Taunton. In fact we went straight to her house and did our school concert starting out from there.

I remember Mr. Nicholson chiefly on account of his "transposing piano"; the whole keyboard could be shifted along sideways, to the maximum space of a major seventh. So indeed, all keys were covered, so to speak, and any transposition was possible. I found it extremely muddling! Of the concert we gave at Taunton School I remember nothing; but we were expected to give our hostess a concert every evening of our stay! It meant a lot of practising; and much time spent hanging around. And then there were horses and Pekinese dogs and a staid butler... I did not manage horse-riding well and I disliked the snuffling dogs. Maurice was far more adaptable, and took kindly to the role of country gentleman. As we had no more school dates in prospect our stay got indefinitely prolonged; I grew weary of it and wanted to be on the road again. Our hostess was certainly kind to us, and most generous, and took us for drives through the surrounding countryside. But these drives were agony for me, for, while driving, she would talk in monologue almost incessantly, sometimes taking both hands off the wheel in order to gesticulate more expressively. Or she would turn around to address the passengers in the back seat! It was terrifying, and I longed for the safety of Mélisande's slow progress. She, however, was perfectly content doing nothing!

In the end we said we must move on: I think we had some idea that we would return to playing in the streets, since the school year was about over. We could expect no more concerts for children. An additional reason for moving on was that Maurice was very keen to walk through Dorset, the home county of his favourite author and namesake, Thomas Hardy. We planned to go via Crewkerne, and then, turning east and south, pass through Dorchester itself, then Tolpuddle and Puddletown. On our first attempt to resurrect the cottage piano on the barrow, we found that it had given up the ghost. It produced only cacophonous clunking sounds and was *so* out of tune as to be completely useless. It could, I suppose, have been used in a pub parlour; and that is where it eventually ended up.

We reached Crewkerne, found ourselves a field to camp in, and repaired to the Antelope for refreshment. Here I tried the great Somerset tipple of draught cider, for the first (and only!) time in my life. It is deceptively mild and exceedingly potent, and our progress later that evening back to the field was erratic; certainly on my part. Later still, I had need to leave the tent, briefly, and discovered in the dark, that our field was full of nettles, which sting most abominably. It was impossible to see them, but they were everywhere!

Maurice and I had had a serious discussion about the immediate future; and about the piano. The country we were about to go through was hilly; we couldn't use the instrument; and what was the point of making poor Mélisande drag the thing around needlessly? We decided to try and sell the piano, walk through Dorset, and then bring our tour to an end. Accordingly, next morning (after the nettles) we went back to the Antelope and persuaded the landlord to buy our piano for sing-songs in his bar; and to our amazement he agreed! We drew up outside the pub, two or three men helped us to take the piano off the barrow and into the inn, and there, for all I know, it may still be. We received thirty shillings for it; as much as we'd paid for Mélisande herself.

She hardly recognized the new, light load that she now pulled; she became positively cheerful and her new-found good spirits were enhanced by meeting a gentleman donkey looking over a gate as we passed by. Of course we had to stop, and he and Mélisande greeted each other courteously, rubbing noses over the low gate. She was quite coy for the rest of the day, and then very companionable in the evening, actually sitting close by us while we had our supper. It was still light, and a bus load of trippers passed along the road by our campsite. When they saw us three, the bus slowed down, and the ill-favoured and bad-mannered occupants gave vent to cat-calls and ribald remarks. This deeply offended Mélisande, as such loutish behaviour was bound to, so she turned her back on them, lifted her tail, and made them a completely appropriate retort. I fear they laughed uproariously; she had unwittingly made their evening for them! But we, in spite of our own laughter, petted her and applauded her ready sense of repartee. We thought the human race had come off second best in that one.

We ambled through Dorset with little fatigue and much pleasure. Our actual end for the Tour was not yet fixed, but when we got to Wareham it was clear there was no point in going further. We had almost reached the sea again. Oddly enough, I can no longer remember what we did with the barrow; but our equipment was sent back to London. For Mélisande, we found what we hoped would be a good home, with a friendly farmer who seemed glad to welcome her. We took a fond farewell of our little brown moke, who had saved our lives in Burford and had proceeded alternately to enchant or to aggravate us; but without whom our Tour would have been impossible.

Two years later Maurice was near Wareham and called at the farm, to learn that poor Mélisande had come to a painful end; she had got at the store of barley meal and had literally eaten herself to death.

Maurice went back to London by train, and I went to join my mother, who was holidaying in the Isle of Wight. But even though the Donkey Tour did not really climax, just petered out, it had proved its worth! In the ensuing four years Maurice and I returned to most of the schools which we had first visited as "The Troubadours", and our clientele broadened each season. Everywhere we went people wanted to know "Where is your donkey now?" When we learned of her death, we both sincerely hoped that there is also a heaven for donkeys, where no pianos have to be hauled along hard roads, and where, however much one eats, one retains one's figure and one's debonair character; and one's digestion!

Our Troubadour days had made many friends for us, for music, and for Mélisande too; and looking back on the adventure after more than half a century, it seems like a story that happened to two other people! The folk at the Royal College of Music had been, it seems, horrified at the idea of two ex-students as penniless tramps, but Maurice's father was able to assure them that we were a success, and making money! And that, after all, is what we all hoped to do with our music; and we were finding audiences to whom what we brought was fresh and interesting. We never played down to the children; never talked down to them either. And I think that, despite all the checks and discomforts which occurred from time to time, neither Maurice nor I have ever regretted the "Donkey Tour".

In 1936 Maurice returned to the West of England, for good, and I joined the staff of the BBC. And as for Mélisande; requiescat in pace.

≡ VI ≡

Back in London

Richard Addinsell. Ivor Novello and "The Happy Hypocrite". The BBC.

*T*HE DONKEY TOUR may have petered out, but we had made many friends and connections. We did have return engagements at many of the places and schools we had formerly visited, and they now paid proper, if modest fees. Even so the number of concerts was by no means enough to live on. Those were pretty lean years.

In 1933 I joined forces with Grahame Clifford, a Lancastrian baritone whom I'd known and liked at R.C.M., and his wife Barbara. We were all poor but thought we might manage better sharing an apartment than living in separate places. We found a ground floor and basement apartment in Earl's Court, clinched the deal with the landlady (who wanted to move out), and she suggested celebrating the transaction with a drink. Unfortunately Mrs. Jenkins's tipple was gin and water; a loathsome mixture, especially at eleven in the morning! But we politely downed our tumblers (Mrs. Jenkins was generous with the gin) and then teetered up the road in great fettle, laughing and shouting with pleasure, towards a little restaurant. By the end of lunch, as we might have known, the joy had worn off and we were all three depressed and fearful. "How shall we ever earn enough on a regular basis to keep paying the rent? We're a trio of fools!"

We did manage though, largely because Barbara, who was a dancer in West End musicals, was never out of work. Grahame and I earned spasmodically. He needed money, if not for himself, certainly for the lovely big Irish setter he and Barbara owned; Jeanne needed meat every day. Grahame and I often got down to our very last coins and would walk round the corner to a butcher's shop and each buy six penn'orth of tripe for our dinner! For those who are unfamiliar with the glories of tripe, it was the very cheapest meat you could buy. Tripe is the lining of a cow's stomach. It is flat, white, flabby meat; about half an inch thick. It makes some people (notably my wife Ishbel) violently ill, but I liked it; cooked, at any rate. Grahame often ate his raw. At the end of the week, on pay-day, Barbara would buy a big bag of groceries and we would have a great feast! Somehow we kept going, and kept pretty cheerful too, most of the time.

I still went to as many concerts as I could, and heard a lot of fine music. One of the most popular chamber-music pairs at this time was a violin-piano duo formed by Jelly d'Aranyi (a grand-niece of Joseph Joachim) and Myra Hess. I had first heard Jelly in 1925 in Manchester, when she played the Mozart _D major Concerto_ with Harty and the Hallé Orchestra. She was a striking woman with jet-black hair, and her dress, with many bright colours and a crinoline skirt, made her look like a gypsy! I was badly smitten (as I had been a year or two earlier by the soprano Elsie Suddaby), and wanted to hear her and Myra play sonatas. Myra was universally loved, all her life, and she was a friend and admirer of my father's. This particular recital at Wigmore Hall was heavily booked, and when I reached the Box Office there were no tickets left under half-a-guinea (ten shillings and sixpence)! I couldn't possibly afford this sum, not even for Jelly and Myra, so I took my courage in both hands, went to the stage door and asked to speak to Miss Hess. When she came, I explained the situation, and asked whether I might be allowed to sit behind the platform, as I had done for the Lener Quartet concerts. She asked Jelly on my behalf, and they let me stay! Not only did I enjoy the music, but I enjoyed seeing these two "great ones" behind the scenes; Myra calm and controlled; Jelly rushing hither and thither in pre-concert excitement. Many years later I mentioned this to Myra, and she said "I may have looked calm, but you've no idea what I felt like inside!"

This little incident was merely one of many which really sprang from being my father's son. Everyone in the profession knew Dad. Because he ran the "Manchester Midday Concerts", many younger artists owed their first Manchester appearance to him. He held auditions every year, both in Manchester and in London, and sometimes in Birmingham too, I think. He was interested in giving young people a chance. The concerts didn't pay fees, but they shared the profits, if any, and the Society absorbed any loss. In any case a Manchester appearance and a Manchester Guardian review were valuable. And artists of the calibre of Myra Hess or Benno Moiseiwitsch would occasionally come up and give a recital which was sure to be sold out, but requiring no share of profits, thus helping the Society greatly.

Of course I still had friends on the staff at R.C.M., but they could not possibly find work for all their former students. So Maurice and I did any odd jobs that came along, and worked to increase our repertoire. Our concerts went well. We played in Manchester, in Dad's Tuesday Midday Concerts, and at many other places in England and Wales. Our favourite schools were those run by the Quakers. Good music seemed to be a part of their general attitude to life. In a year or two, we were ready to play at Wigmore Hall[11].

I got a few engagements on my own; notably in Birmingham with Leslie Heward who was then the conductor of the City of Birmingham Orchestra. He was an enormously gifted and musical man, and I thoroughly enjoyed playing the Schumann *Concerto* under his deeply sympathetic direction. I'd already played the Beethoven *1st Concerto* with him, and the following year I risked the *Emperor*. But I wasn't ready for it and the performance was disappointing.

In 1935 a thing happened to me which affected the course of my life more than I could possibly have foreseen. My former teacher, the composer Gordon Jacob (whose *First Piano Concerto* I had had so much fun with at a Bournemouth Symphony Concert) sent me word of a man who was wanting some help with orchestration. This turned out to be none other than Richard Addinsell, soon to be so very famous as the composer of the *Warsaw Concerto*. His need was actually for a sort of musical amanuensis. He knew what he wanted to write, and how he wanted to hear it, but he needed someone to do the writing and scoring for him. I went to work with him on a score of incidental music for *Alice in Wonderland*, and I found it completely different from any music with which I'd previously had experience. This was the start of a long collaboration; we worked together on a good many scores. I grew very

fond of Dick; and he was extraordinarily good to me. I began to appre-
ciate his sense of the theatre, and his knack of finding just the right type
of melody or atmosphere for a given passage in a play or film. I enjoyed
orchestrating his music, which I would already have taken down in
shorthand from his playing of it on the piano. Altogether I gained a deal
of knowledge and experience; not least from hearing what I had scored
when it was played at the recording session! These recording sessions
would be conducted by another old R.C.M. friend, Muir Mathieson.
He did an exceptionally good job for London Films and for British
composers, beginning with Arthur Bliss, whose music for the H.G. Wells
film *The Shape of Things to Come* pioneered good music in films. Muir
went on to engage other serious composers for films, such as Vaughan
Williams, John Ireland (who was not a great success), William Alwyn, and
many others.

Dick Addinsell was a wonderful jazz pianist, as many others, including Joyce Grenfell, have attested. His playing was gentle and musical, full
of life and very appealing. And so relaxed; so easy! At one a.m. after a
long evening's work, to listen to him play was a marvelous restorer. Dick
often collaborated with the author Clemence Dane, so I was fortunate
therefore in getting to know this great lady, known to her friends as
Winifred Ashton. Once, I had the delightful experience of playing to her
and Gladys Stern ("G.B. Stern"), both of them lying on the floor, so they
could relax. I played on for an hour or more. Not jazz; I can't play it at
all; but Bach and Chopin and Debussy: and they were refreshed and
invigorated by it. So was I! I went wherever Dick and Winifred might
be working, in town or in the country; and simply stayed and worked.
I was fed and housed, and each time it was a tonic to me, however hard
I had to work.

Dick's music was derivative but apt, and he wrote the music for a
number of good films; *Fire Over England, Blithe Spirit, South Riding,* and
Dangerous Moonlight among them. Late in 1935 he and Clemence Dane
started on an adaptation of Max Beerbohm's *The Happy Hypocrite.* It was
to be a spoken play with almost continuous incidental music under the
dialogue. We scored it for an orchestra of 17 players, and I became fascinated with it. The music was good, the problems of scoring were
intriguing, and the story was charming: a loutish Regency beau becomes

enamoured of a little dancing girl at Vauxhall Gardens, but he is so gross and ugly she will have nothing to do with him. His name is "Lord George Hell". The little girl's effect on him is such that he gives up his life of debauchery and goes to live simply and rustically in Kensington. This new life changes his face and his figure; clean and beautiful, he again approaches his Jenny, now under the name of "George Heaven". He wins her and she goes to live with him in rural bliss. Together they put to flight his late mistress, an Italian actress, and the whole thing ends in a sentimental "happily-ever-after" atmosphere.

The script and music caught the eye of one of England's matinée idols, Ivor Novello. Normally he wrote his own shows, words and music, and won all hearts by triumphing over every evil and ending wholly victorious. But the idea of George Hell with a hideous face becoming the saintly George Heaven, appealed to him. For George Hell he would be suitably made up; for George Heaven, instead of the mask of beauty he is supposed to buy in Bond Street and wear to beguile Jenny, Ivor would simply wear his own face. He was a very handsome man!

Ivor agreed to produce *The Happy Hypocrite*, and for his Jenny he chose the young and delicious Vivien Leigh, then just at the start of her career. And so, it soon went into rehearsal. For conductor they engaged a man whom I had known at R.C.M. who was now associated with Covent Garden. But the business of matching the music to the dialogue was tricky; the tempi had to be exactly right, so that the music was at a given place by the time a certain sentence was reached. And that had to happen continuously, throughout the piece, so that one was always at the right spot at the right moment, and so that changes in musical texture would have their proper effect and fit in with the movement on stage.

The poor conductor had no sense of pace, and was never in the right spot; it was aggravating, and indeed frightening to listen to. I attended most rehearsals, in case I was needed. The show was to play a week in Southport and then a week in Manchester before opening in London at His Majesty's Theatre. At the last London rehearsal before going to Southport, Ivor Novello dismissed the conductor. There was an interval of agitated conference backstage, but there was only one other person besides the composer who knew the score well, and that person was I. And so, Ivor sent for me and asked if I would be the conductor. It was a marvelous windfall and I jumped at the opportunity! I knew every note of the score; hadn't I written it *all* down? And I loved the show. I wanted a success for all concerned. I had been most impressed with Ivor Novello; I had expected some airs of a "grandee" from him but there never were *any*. He worked harder at rehearsal than any of his cast; he was always early in attendance and the last away. No detail escaped him and into the bargain he was sensitive and musical: a joy to work with.

Thus I was back in the theatre. We had one orchestral rehearsal in Southport, no dress rehearsal, and I was tipped in at the deep end! Once I got over my initial nervousness I enjoyed every performance. Never were two successive nights the same; one followed the actors' speeds and movements, so one had to be on the "qui vive" the whole time. Ivor had one particular long monologue, and he never spoke it the same two nights running; but he was a fine artist, and I could always sense what he was going to do.

We came to London after two quite good weeks in Lancashire, and for eight more weeks I had a job which I liked immensely, and a salary! But *The Happy Hypocrite* was just too sentimental for the Stalls, and not quite Novello-ish enough for the Gallery, and so it lasted only a short run. I was sad to say goodbye to the show and the cast; to the members of my orchestra and to Ivor Novello, whom I never met again. But I had indeed had a most exhilarating musical and human experience.

Since I first came to London in 1925, and for a couple of years before that too, the biggest purveyor of music for the general public was the British Broadcasting Corporation (originally Company). Its head was the Scotsman Sir John Reith (later Lord Reith). There is an amusing and not wholly unlifelike imitation of him in Nevil Shute's wartime novel *No Highway*, in the person of an irascible and gifted aircraft designer. However, Sir John designed no aircraft; he did design a fine and national broadcast service, which fulfilled all everyone's expectations in wartime.

My father had been one of the first pianists to play for the BBC, from 1923 onwards. Some artists were a little hesitant at first about this newfangled "wireless", but Dad's name became very well-known as a broadcaster, even after he had lost his sight. And I got to know some of the BBC staff who looked after music broadcasts in Manchester, notably

Albert Jordan, 1880. Maternal grandfather.

Emma Jordan, 1884. Maternal grandmother.

Carl Fuchs (uncle), 1865-1951 (photo: 1921).

Dʳ Adolf Brodsky

Dr. Adolf Brodsky, 1851-1929 (photo: c. 1905)

(Left) Isaacs family (1910). Back row: Stella Isaacs,
Great-grandfather Harris, Amy Isaacs.
Front row: Edward Isaacs (holding Leonard),
Annie Isaacs (grandmother).

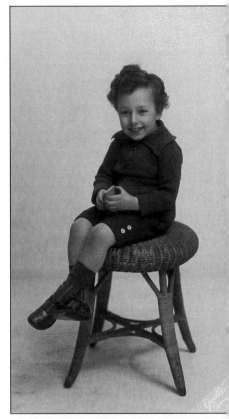

Leonard, aged 1¹/2, with mother Amy (late 1910)

Leonard, aged 4¹/2 (1913)

The Cousins (Fuchs, Jordan and Isaacs children, 1920). From left to right: Hwat (the dog), Betty Jordan, Ruth Isaac
Stanley Jordan, Charles Jordan, Leonard Isaacs, Marjorie Jordan, Elaine Jordan, Edgar Fuchs. (Arnold Fuchs is takin,
the photo)

Family Group, 1921 or 1922. Back row: Francis Jordan, Edward Isaacs, Amy Isaacs, (Tante) Wally Fuchs, Franz Loewenthal, Carl Fuchs. Middle row: Elaine Jordan, Daisy Jordan, Alf Jordan, Christine Jordan, Nelly Fuchs, Leonard Isaacs, Rose Jordan. Front row: Edgar Fuchs, Stanley Jordan, Ruth Isaacs, Betty Jordan, Charles Jordan, Marjorie Jordan (and Hwat, the dog!).

STRANDED ENGLISH OPERA COMPANY

Picture shows part of the stranded English Light Opera company, taken on the steps of Grace church by the e Press photographer this morning. Front row shows Haigh Jackson, Dorothy Croft, Olive Hemingway, with ry Jaxon, musical director, in the centre. Immediately behind Mr. Jaxon is Mrs. Jaxon. At the back are: adoline Evans, Molly Elvar, Leonard Isaacs, Barry Sherriff, Alec Morphy, Dorothy George, Clare Bayliss and ell Durran.

Leonard with French Horn,
Royal College of Music, 1927.   *The English Light Opera Company in Winnipeg, February, 1932.*

Rival to Modestine

EVERY listener knows Edward Isaacs The Manchester pianist has given many microphone recitals. He has also invented a writing device to help out his own failing sight. Recently, through the medium of these columns, he offered to share this device

'Travelled through the Western countries'

with any blind listeners who might be interested. He received many hundreds of replies. Few listeners yet know Edward's pianist son Leonard, who broadcast from Manchester a fortnight ago. This summer Leonard Isaacs and Maurice Hardy, the 'cellist, loaded a piano on a donkey-cart and travelled through the Western counties playing in their streets. They played popular stuff, but no jazz. Local girls' schools occasionally invited them in to give sonata recitals. Head mistresses were hospitable, let the vagabonds camp in the grounds, offered them the bathroom—while the girls were at breakfast. The donkey was called Mélisande. A friendly landlord, mistaking them for tramps, stood them a meal. Later he bought the piano, which now reposes in a Somerset pub. Mélisande they sold in Dorset. She appeared none the worse for her four months of Brahms, Debussy, and Chopin. A good adventure, this, recalling Robert Louis Stevenson and his donkey Modestine.

Leonard, Mélisande, and Maurice Hardy, May 1932

(Right) Radio Times, October 7, 1932

Edward Isaacs (now blind) and Leonard, 1936.

Call-up! 1942. Leonard is front row, extreme left.

Marianne Bardas, c. 1942

Naomi and Nicholas Isaacs, c. 1950

Ishbel MacDonald, Ottawa, Canada, 1957.

Gordon Clinton (baritone) and Leonard Isaacs, taken in Canada, 1953.

Nicholas Isaacs and his wife Tian-En Yu, mid 1990.

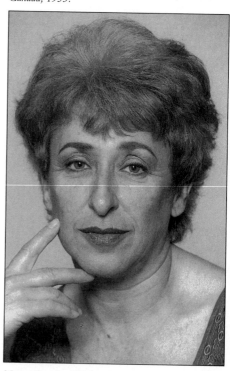

Naomi Isaacs, c. 1996

Margaret and Debbie Isaacs at Blue Sea Lake, c. 1970

Harry Scherman (second cousin) 1969, New York City.

Leonard in academic gown at University of Manitoba, 1967.

Prof. L. Isaacs, director of the School of Music, will retire at the end of August after 11 years with the university. A reception in his honor was held recently in Pembina Hall. He was presented with a recording of Mozart's 10 last string quartets performed by the Amadeus Quartet and a cheque toward the purchase of Groves Dictionary of Music (10 volumes).

Leonard and Ishbel at L.'s retirement reception, 1974.

Debbie Isaacs, college graduation, 1990

Margaret Isaacs, 1995

Ishbel, Leonard, and Audrey and Herb Belyea, on cruise to Alaska, August, 1997.

Leonard in his favourite chair at home, November 1997.

Kenneth Wright, who had been an engineer but who went over to music. He was near the top of the BBC Manchester hierarchy. A few years later, while I was still at college in London, I broadcast too; Kenneth Wright had been transferred to London, where he eventually became Assistant Head of Music.

In 1928 I discovered the keyboard music of Bach's sons Carl Philipp Emanuel, Wilhelm Friedemann, and Johann Christian. The BBC engaged me, at my suggestion, to give short recitals of this music, one every evening for a week, in the famous "Recitals F" series. I was still on the BBC's books after 1930, when I ceased to be a full-time student, and I did the occasional broadcast. Even then, it seemed to me that a position on the staff would be very welcome, should one ever materialize.

In 1935 I came across the first four *Songs and Dances (Cançós i Dansas)* by the Catalan composer Federico Mompou. I thought them really charming (I still do!) and set about orchestrating them. I secured the composer's approval and took the scores to show to my old teacher Sir Adrian Boult, who was the BBC's Director of Music and its Chief Conductor. He liked the scores, and performed the pieces with the BBC Symphony Orchestra. This made me bold enough to ask if there would be a possible place for me on the staff. But there was not. They thought my experience was inadequate, and it probably was. But Kenneth Wright told me that there might be a position in "Light Music", and that I should keep on trying.

Incidentally, in order to have Mompou's approval of my orchestrations I had gone to Paris, where he lived, and taken the scores with me for him to see. I had an appointment to call on him one morning at 11 o'clock, and duly presented myself at his apartment. I was shown into the Salon, and there I waited for a whole hour! At noon he came in; tall and thin, with a most charming manner. He apologized for keeping me waiting (he was still in his dressing gown) "but" he said, "I do find it so difficult to get up in the mornings!" He liked the scores and got his publishers' permission for them to be played. Many years later we met again, in a BBC studio where he and his wife performed his songs and piano music in a broadcast recital.

In 1936 *The Happy Hypocrite* had given me a taste of what it was like to earn a weekly salary. For ten weeks it had been very reassuring! After it came to an end I went back to see Kenneth Wright, to ask once more for a job. "What have you been doing lately?" he asked. "Well" I replied, "I've just been conducting a show for Ivor Novello...." "Oh! Have you? Just wait a minute; I'll go in and see the Director." After a few minutes he came back to his office and invited me to go in and see Sir Adrian. In the result, I came away with a job; Programme Assistant in Light Music; starting in October at five pounds a week! And from October 1936 until June 1963; with an interval of two and a half years during the war; I was a "corporation servant". It seemed, and was, a fluke, but a most fortunate one, for the following years were very full indeed and mostly very interesting.

Arranging programmes of Light Music brought me into contact with a repertoire, and with performers, all previously outside my experience: Troise and his Mandoliers; Medvedeff and his Balalaika Orchestra; Mantovani (before he became so famous); Leslie Bridgewater and his two Quintets, one piano and strings; the other violin, cello, flute, oboe and harp. The latter ensemble was fascinating! All five players were "stars" (Jean Pougnet, Anthony Pini, Arthur Gleghorn, Leon Goossens, and John Cockerill) and the performances were immaculate. Bridgewater had me make some arrangements for them and it was a joy to do so. Then I found myself in charge of cinema organ broadcasts; an instrument which I loathed, and a set of players all new to me, and not always too skilled. The cinema organ was a feature of the days of silent films; in the bigger movie theatres a large organ would be installed, usually one which could be made to rise out of a pit, and subside again. The organist would be required to accompany the films with suitable music; and also, once during each show would be raised from his pit to entertain the audience with some solos. Though some of the players were very good indeed, the repertoire was of the most brainless popular type! In the years before the Talkies, they were a regular part of theatre life, and were broadcast almost every day! There was at least one player whose technique was above reproach and who also showed real musical taste, Quentin Maclean. He used to put Mozart overtures into his broadcast programmes, and played them well. Unfortunately this encouraged the others who were not such good players, to do the same, with sometimes disastrous results for the music. I invited Maclean in one day for a cup of coffee, explained the situation to him, and asked if he would abstain from playing such famous orchestral pieces. His reply was quite reasonable, and unanswerable: "Well, if I can play them, I don't see why I shouldn't." (He might have added that G.D. Cunningham did precisely the same sort of thing in the Town Hall Birmingham, in his midday recitals.) I was worsted, and didn't cross swords with a cinema organist again! In any case, as I grew a bit wiser, my opinion of them as a genus improved somewhat.

The BBC possessed its own theatre organ and a resident staff player, Reginald Foort, whom I got to know quite well, and liked, too. He was outside my jurisdiction, since he belonged not to Music Department, but to Variety Department. In the first war he had served in submarines, and once took me down to the London docks where a sub, manned by acquaintances of his, was in port. We visited with them, which involved drinking gin at 2 o'clock in the afternoon, in the smallest mess-room one could imagine: even my 5'3" was too tall for the low ceiling! The rest of the afternoon was one great headache!

The BBC was divided into departments, each responsible for its par-ticular contributions to the Controller of the Service being supplied; Home, Light Programme, Overseas, and later, Third Programme. Each department had its own head, and there was also, naturally, a big Engineering Department. The "RadioTimes", a weekly programme journal, and its more intellectual counterpart "The Listener" were run by their own staffs, with a representative in each department. The Radio Times was a periodical of the accuracy of which we were all proud. It had to be accurate, and a misprint or an error in R.T. was a terrible offence, of which one heard and felt the repercussions for weeks! There were a considerable number of programme departments; Music, Variety, Talks, Features, Religion, Drama, Children's Hour, News.... I no longer remember them all! Then of course, there were departments which dealt with Contracts and Finance, and the Administration (or "Manage-ment"). During my first while in the Corporation I worked inside the Music Department and came little into contact with the wider author-ities of the BBC. I simply arranged those broadcasts of which I was in charge, and saw to it that the details were correct when they were sent to Radio Times. My immediate boss at first, was a tall dreamy man called

Horace Dann, and the office had one secretary, Dorothea Pritchett. She was a highly efficient and sharp-tongued lady who ran the Light Music of the BBC with an iron hand. *No* detail escaped her; she read the rules to all contributing bands and ensembles, and indeed all of them seemed to regard her with some awe. She, rather than Dann, taught me the workings of the department, and I was always grateful to her for saving me from committing crimes against the Administration!

All programmes for a given week were supposed to be in by a certain date, and on the penultimate day each office would be visited by another competent sharp-tongued lady, demanding late programmes within 24 hours, "or else". This was Hilda Bennett, whose job was to see *all* programme information through to Radio Times, to the Announcers, to the Engineering Departments who would have to see it onto the air, to Copyright and Library, and to any other people who had any relations at all with the music programmes. I started my BBC life with a healthy fear of Miss Bennett, but as time went by, and the War caused us all to come much closer together, I grew very fond of her. Her impatience and her humour and her basic kindliness were characteristic of that part of the country where she and I had both been born, Lancashire. After her retirement Hilda married and had some years of great happiness with her Harry (Luscombe). My wife and I mourned her when, far too young, she passed on.

Each week in the Music Department there were two Departmental meetings, known as "Artists Committee" at which the department head and all programme builders reviewed past programmes, discussed future ones, and heard reports on the performances of broadcasting artists and of the most recent auditions. These meetings were also attended by a gentleman called "Artists' Booking Manager", who saw to the issue of all artists' contracts, and kept an eye on the equitable distribution of engagements inside the musical profession. And, though the profession often complained, he (at that time Arthur Wynn, a retired operatic baritone) did a very fair job. All performers "on the books" could reasonably expect a certain number of dates in a year, even if only one. Arthur Wynn kept tally (as did his successor Norman Carrell) and would remind us if Mr. X or Miss Y were being forgotten. The BBC had by this time a huge influence on the musical profession, and it was known that certain very moderate performers regarded their annual broadcast as a sort of guarantee of keeping their pupils or acquiring new ones. Arthur Wynn acted as a benevolent guardian of these people's rights.

After a while I began to realise how big a responsibility we carried, and I tried, all through the years, to discharge it fairly. One is bound to be, to some extent, subjective where the performance of music is concerned (especially if one is, oneself, a performer), but given a reliable degree of competence, performers were entitled to their appearances, once the BBC had formally inscribed their names on the list of available artists. This applied, too, to people resident in other parts of the country than London. The BBC had stations in Glasgow, Edinburgh, Belfast, Cardiff, Bristol, Newcastle, Manchester and Birmingham; and although these stations broadcast local programmes and had lists of artists selected for regional broadcasts, there were many musicians of national status resident in the provinces (my father was one such) whose interests had to be viewed both locally and from London.

My colleagues included Eric Warr, who had come to London via the Birmingham offices, and with whom I'd been at school in Manchester; Maurice Johnstone, whom I'd also known in Manchester where he had kept a music store; Clarence Raybould and Joseph Lewis, both conductors; Anthony Lewis, who after the War became the first Music Organiser to the Third Programme and later still, Principal of the Royal Academy of Music; Herbert Murrill, the composer, whom I already knew; St. George Phillips, who looked after chamber music programmes; Julian Herbage, the Senior Programme Builder; W. W. Thompson, the Concerts Manager; the Assistant Head, Kenneth Wright; and of course Sir Adrian Boult, Head of the Department and Conductor of the BBC Symphony Orchestra (which had been founded in 1930). Harold Rutland was the music man for Radio Times, and the delightful Rollo Myers for The Listener. Besides these people, there were the Programme Engineers, who created the microphone balance in the studio and who were always represented at departmental meetings. Joining the department at almost the same time as Herbert Murrill and myself was Dr. Reginald Thatcher (later Sir Reginald), who came to us from Harrow School and went on sometime later to the Royal Academy of Music. It was a variegated collection of people and tastes, and on the whole we did, I think, provide a well-balanced diet for the listener.

During the time I was in Light Music I got to know that beautiful violinist Alfredo Campoli. He was one of Leslie Bridgewater's musicians, and played in studio ensembles and the theatres of the West End. But he tired of playing salon pieces and fireworks, retired for a couple of years, and emerged as a "virtuoso", playing the big repertoire with an impeccable technique and fine interpretative powers. He had thereafter a most distinguished career. Maybe thirty years later he came to Winnipeg, at my invitation, and we played two concerts together at the University of Manitoba. We played Franck, Busoni, Dvořák and Beethoven, and it afforded me the greatest possible pleasure. Alfredo also played bridge in any bit of spare time!

After about a couple of years of Light Music I was glad to be transferred to "serious" recitals. I found myself more or less in my own repertoire, so to speak, but not entirely. I was again in charge of organ recitals, but this time church organs. I spent many a lunch hour attending organ recitals in city churches, to learn the repertoire, so that, hopefully, I could meet and talk with organists without making too big a fool of myself! I found some attractive and friendly people in this part of the profession, until now hardly known to me at all; and fine musicians into the bargain. John Dykes Bower of Durham Cathedral and later St. Paul's; Harold Darke of St. Michael's Cornhill; Thalben Ball of the Temple Church; Arnold Richardson of Wolverhampton; G.D. Cunningham of Birmingham Town Hall; C.H. Trevor; Charles Spinks of St. Luke's Chelsea; and that dear man Guy Weitz of Farm Street. A few years later I met some fine visiting organists from the continent; André Marchal, Maurice Duruflé, Gunther Ramin from Leipzig; the redoubtable Fernando Germani from Rome. The most remarkable was Marchal, who was blind, but who in a few minutes familiarized himself with the BBC's big 4-manual Compton with "touch-stops" which lighted up when pressed and had to be pressed again to be cancelled. It was amazing to watch him finding his way in this labyrinth of little lights, of which he could, of course, see nothing. He did not risk giving a recital on this instrument, but used the older and more traditional one at Maurice Vinden's church of St. Mark, North Audley Street. Like pretty well all the French organists who visited us, Marchal was piloted and looked after by Felix Aprahamian. He wasn't in their employ; this was all done voluntarily, out of devotion to the organists and their music. No organ recital anywhere in London was complete without Felix's presence.

My occupation with recitals soon embraced far more than just organ programmes. I began to deal with all kinds; piano, violin, song, and chamber music too. The senior of our office was Anthony Lewis[12], of whom I stood in some awe. He never admitted to ignorance of any musical fact whatsoever; was never "caught out"; and could be quite caustic. I found this hard to accept at first, as he was 6 years my junior in arithmetical age! But he mellowed; or else I became less edgy; and I became fond of him. My admiration of his scholarship was considerable, and genuine; and he reciprocated by liking my Debussy-playing. That was a compliment after my own heart! In the same office were Herbert Murrill, who later became Head of Music and who died far too young, in 1952; and that dear muddle-headed amateur cellist St. George Phillips. All in all, 1938 and the first months of 1939 were peaceful and enjoyable, musically; and in spite of the Anschluss and Munich we kept hoping, but I think everyone knew that the false peace was bound to be shattered before too long.

≡VII≡
World War Two. Bristol.
RAF Band and Orchestra.
The Pottsdam Conference.

A ND SHATTERED IT WAS! I happened to be in Broadcasting House when Neville Chamberlain made his announcement of the declaration of war against Germany. I stood in a studio, along with a few other people, and listened to him. Then, almost coinciding with the end of the broadcast, came the air-raid sirens! Those caught in the corridors made bee-lines for the nearest studio, as we had been told to do; I remember seeing the announcer who had just introduced the Prime Minister, making such a dash. And then we waited. After a while we realized that it had been a false alarm, but later on we got all too accustomed to that awful wailing sound!

For the first few days of war the atmosphere was unreal. The Governors of the BBC (all apparently Blimps from another age) prohibited all serious, or even decent, music; we were all to live on a diet of military marches played by service bands and brass bands! It was quite awful. Endless, mindless military music, punctuated by news bulletins with nothing in them! After a few days of this, the Great British Public made itself heard. The screams of rage came from every quarter of the country, and soon, shyly, the strains of Vaughan Williams's *Greensleeves* came out of our loudspeakers, and the hiatus was over. The Governors had indeed miscalculated very badly. No one wanted to, or could, go back to the days of the First War, and that sort of jingoistic nonsense was dead for good and all. The public appetite for real music increased throughout the war, and it was a worthwhile job being part of the mechanism by which it was purveyed. Concerts in factories, and Myra Hess's

famous National Gallery Concerts were all a part of it. It was received
with much approval and delight when it became known that the Queen
would slip along, incognito, to the Gallery, and sit with Myra backstage
during many a concert.

We knew at the BBC that some scheme of decentralization was
planned for us, and very soon we got our marching orders. Music
Department was being transferred, lock, stock and barrel, to Bristol. *We*
supposed that someone had imagined that the Germans wouldn't know
where Bristol was, but they did, and surely let us know that they did! At
first though, everything was quiet. We all found ourselves somewhere to
live, made the acquaintance of our regular Bristol colleagues who ran the
BBC's West Region, and started to turn a private home in Pembroke
Road, Clifton, into a set of offices. The BBC Symphony Orchestra and
Sir Adrian had also been evacuated to Bristol, and we soon became more
of a family than had ever been the case in London.

It was not long before a detachment of the Home Guard was formed.
It was an amusing, if not too inspiring, sight to observe the Orchestra
marching along Whiteladies Road, headed by Sir Adrian and his
adjutant, Mr. Ernest Hall (the Principal Trumpet), all in fine-looking
uniforms; except right at the rear, the poor tympanist in "civvies". He
was too stout to have yet found a uniform which fitted him! The Home
Guard did guard duty and other quasi-military things. It seemed rather
silly at the time, mounting an armed guard outside Broadcasting House
when there was no sign whatsoever of any parachutists. I recall with
some chagrin being detailed to stand at the front door of Broadcasting
House with a loaded rifle which I had *no* idea how to use; and while
there, greeting my good friends Bill Pleeth and his wife Margaret Good
who had come to do a broadcast. Their incredulity and laughter was
considerable, and recurred whenever we met thereafter! I am really not
a military type!

Then again, at the bottom of the garden of our office-house was a
small transmitting aerial; so of course we had to mount not only a Fire-
guard but a Home Guard too, every night. One night when it was my
turn to be the Home Guard on duty, I was sitting in the transmitter
room, somewhere around 2:30 a.m., quietly reading a book, with my
rifle propped up in the corner (yes, still loaded). Not a sound to be

heard; the Fire Guards were all snoring upstairs in the guard-room; when suddenly I became aware of a small but quite regular flopping sound, gradually approaching. Now, the transmitter room was on ground level, reached by a passage from the back door, which gave onto the garden. So, rather gingerly I picked up the rifle and stole out into the passage to see what sort of a German infiltrator I might meet. And there, approaching me in small hops, was a little green frog. His jumps were quite loud in the silent night. I'd no idea what to do with a small frog in the wee hours, so I let him hop into the transmitter room and hide under one of the big pieces of apparatus. And there he stayed; I don't know for how long! I duly reported the occurrence to the Officer of the Guard, my colleague Arthur Wynn, and a night or two later, when next on duty, I looked in the log-book and found the entry "November 10th, 4:00 a.m.; Isaacs caught a frog".

We had another contretemps there too. One of our number had fixed up trip-wires in the front and back gardens, and connected them to warning buzzers in the guard-room, suitably labelled "front" and "back". One night one of these buzzers suddenly sounded off! Consternation! What are we to do now? Panic! No instructions of any kind were to be found in the duty sheets, so not feeling very brave, we rang up the nearest other Home Guard post, and reported. Soon there was a heavy knock at the front door. Dr. Thatcher and a posse of his troops were there, all complete in tin hats, with bayonets fixed! They "deployed" into the garden and found... nothing at all except a pulled-up trip-wire. Nobody to be seen; not even the cat which had caused the trouble! But they did find that the trip-wires had been wrongly connected, and "front" meant "back" and "back" meant "front"! They were promptly disconnected, and never used again; while Harry Vowles, whose bright idea it had been, kept a discreet silence for a long time thereafter.

There was, of course, also the serious business of broadcasting to be attended to. Not only were programmes to be arranged in advance, as was customary, but it was found advisable to meet the artists arriving in Bristol by train, and see them to their hotels. The blackout, as well as possible traffic diversions, made it necessary. For the concerts, one large studio was available at Bristol's Broadcasting House in Whiteladies Road, and one or two others were put into commission in church halls. The old anonymity of the Programme Builder disappeared; we found it necessary, and also very pleasant to be present at the broadcasts we had arranged. Odd jobs might be needed, like turning pages for an accompanist, or just giving general support when no personal friends were available. Occasionally it was a very good thing one of us was there, if only to see our performer back to his or her hotel. You never knew for certain, once we had reached the stage of almost-nightly air-raids, whether or not the hotel would even still be there!

One evening, just about 6:00 p.m. (the time at which the sirens usually sounded the warning) the pianist Iso Elinson was in the big studio at Broadcasting House, about to embark upon the twelve Chopin *Études, opus 25*, when the sirens did go off. The studio roof had been somewhat strengthened, but it would be no match for a bomb, so we asked Elinson if he wished to play, or to go to shelter and we would put on records. His reply was "Hitler has banned Chopin in Poland, but it's not banned *here*; I'm playing!" Elinson always made himself as comfortable as possible for a broadcast; jacket thrown on one side, suspenders slipped off, lights dimmed; so, we went through the usual drill. There we were, Elinson, the announcer Peter Fettes, and I; and the recital went ahead. Elinson even had the presence of mind to keep his right foot on the sustaining pedal in between pieces, so that the piano sound rang; thereby a possible thump of a falling bomb might be dulled "over the air". It was a 40 minute recital, and halfway through a man in a tin hat came into the studio and whispered, somewhat hoarsely, "Are you on the air?" Peter nodded, whereupon the man said "Christ, they're falling in the garden now!" and withdrew. Well, Elinson finished in great style; he didn't turn a hair; and yet I knew him in civilian life as a highly nervous and jumpy person. This sang-froid was quite astonishing, and impressive. His reward was to lose all his luggage in the hotel where he'd booked in; very little of that hotel was left standing.

Buildings disappeared, overnight, and the constant smell of burning was very unpleasant. A particularly good sherry bar went up in smoke one night. I think it was called the Posada; it had been a lovely warm place to meet for a while in an evening. They had sawdust on the floor; the place was divided into partial compartments, and only wine-drinkers were allowed past the first compartment! Those wanting beer or whiskey had to stay by the door. The sherry was all in casks, straight off the boat from Spain. The host would make up a blend on the spot, for you to try. We missed that bar very much indeed: the sherry all ran away into the drains and the gutters.

There was a big concert-hall in Bristol, the Colston Hall. Here the Symphony Orchestra made its home, and gave public concerts through all the time I was in Bristol. The London artists, and others, got quite used to the journey, and to being collected from their trains and escorted to their hotels. The blackout made this absolutely necessary, and one could also be "caught out" by the air-raid. I remember spending a whole evening and half the night too, in the basement of the Royal Hotel, along with a host of other folk, including the very popular light tenor Webster Booth and his wife, the soprano Anne Ziegler! For people coming by road, and a few did venture, the blackout difficulties were increased, and it was unwise to try and cover too much ground by car. The pianist Irene Scharrer somehow came to be in Bristol with a car, and I remember being driven by her, from a church studio back to Broadcasting House, in the dark, and she drove between a lamp-standard and the wall at the inner edge of the sidewalk! How she did it was never clear to either of us!

The members of staff who made up the West Region of the BBC became our good friends, amongst them Reginald (Rex) Redman, the head of Music, and his wife, the pianist Evelyn Amey. Also Bristol's indefatigable and first-rate accompanist Winifred Davey, who subsequently transferred to London. And very much to the front of Bristolian activities were their two announcers Peter Fettes and Hugh Shirreff. Not only music went on from the Bristol studios; there was a wonderfully funny show called *Danger Men at Work*, the forerunner of ITMA[13], which was produced there by the energetic and delightful Max Kester. The humour was Marxian, and I tried never to miss a broadcast. During one particularly long air-raid, I spent a whole night on the stairs at Broadcasting House with the female star of the show, Doris Nicholls!

One got quite used to the raids, though always hoping that the bombs would go to the side. One night, during a raid which started promptly at 6:00 p.m., considerable damage was being done in Clifton, that part of Bristol where our offices were. We were all still there; there'd been no time to pack up and go home. Some of the secretaries took shelter across the road in a big house where several members of staff were billetted. The house belonged to Lady Barron, a rather marvelous old lady who was the widow of a surgeon who had been Lord Mayor of Bristol on more than one occasion. She was quite imperturbable, and was very angry that Hitler should cause her to consider moving her customary dinner hour, or to move out of the ground-floor room where she was wont to dine. Her housekeeper persuaded her to be a bit prudent, and that very evening the house next door was hit by a bomb. Lady Barron and whoever was dining with her that evening dived under the table! When the sound of falling masonry had subsided, Lady Barron remarked, in a completely unmoved voice "You know, it's only when you get really near to it, that you see how threadbare this carpet has become"! Well, on the night of the early raid of which I was speaking a moment ago, two or three of us stayed on in the office. I suspect we were on "fire-watch", and before long there was a call from Lady Barron's. Pamela Young, one of our secretaries, reported an incendiary bomb on the roof, and "could someone please come over and put it out?"

Basil Douglas and I collected buckets and stirrup pumps and went across the road. Fires burning everywhere, and the constant sound of planes and bombs exploding, and the sirens still at it too!! It was a matter of less than a hundred yards to the house. We were met at the front door by Lady Barron herself, holding a candle which she shaded with her other hand: "So kind of you to come round", she said, "You'll find the fire on the second floor". Actually we didn't find it at all, because it had already been extinguished by Ambrose Gauntlett, the principal cellist of the Symphony, and his son. So Basil and I left, and walked up the road to where the big church immediately opposite our offices was now ablaze. We went to see if we could give any help, though firemen were already there in great numbers.

It looked very like my idea of Hell; the sky was livid with fire, the flames from the burning church were towering up in the air, and the noise was constant and deafening. We found we could in fact be of some assistance to the firemen, who were from Cardiff as well as Bristol; we could spell them off for a few minutes every so often. That's the only time I have ever held a full-size fire hose; it was heavy, and quite a challenge to try and aim straight into the flames where the fireman directed me. The church was streaming with water and alight with fire, everywhere, at the same time; highly melodramatic! Then, into this inferno walked a man carrying a tray with a big jug of tea on it, and a collection of mugs: "I saw you chaps workin' away; I thought as how you might like a drop of tea." Marvelous! No covering, no tin hat, no protection; simply camaraderie and goodwill!

By this time (it must have been well into 1940, for the "phoney war" was over) I was living in a big old house in Royal York Crescent, along with other BBC types; Hilda Bennett, the principal flute Gerald Jackson and his rather deaf wife; and Eric Pritchard, the second trumpet and later on tympanist. Hilda had a kitten and the Jacksons a dog. We also had a very deep cellar, but to go there during a raid was worse than staying upstairs. Gerald fussed and worried, his wife kept saying "Was that a bomb, dear?", the dog chased the kitten and Eric practised side drum on his heel! Hilda and I preferred to stand at the front door, from which we had a superb view, and watch the flares coming down and the explosions going up. We were very lucky not to have been hit, for that terrace of houses must have been highly visible from the air. The only BBC casualty of whom we heard was the bass player Cockerill, brother of the harpist John Cockerill.

Occasionally someone we knew well would come down from London and Hilda and I would arrange a party. Once the cellist Antoni Sala came, straight from his garden in, I think, Fittleworth (West Sussex) and brought "goodies". He made the most wonderful stew of chicken, broad beans, small Spanish sausages called chulichos and lashings of olive oil. It was toothsome, and very different from our normal diet. Ever since then I have cooked my stews on a basis of olive oil, and remember Toni Sala with gratitude and pleasure. He was a nice cellist too. The fourth member of the party that evening was another cellist, Hilda's and my colleague St. George Phillips. He was finding the war and the conditions in Bristol very wearing. He didn't have enough to do, and found not being in London extremely stressful. He was, not long after, put "on leave" and went back to London; the BBC had had from him what he could give.

Otherwise the Bristol contingent of Music Department was much what it had been in London. But all of Light Music had been sent to a different base, near Evesham. There stayed the Salon Orchestra with Stanford Robinson, Kenneth Wright, Leslie Bridgewater; and it was years before we saw them again, except on fleeting visits. I do not know what had happened to Rollo Myers at that time; the next time I saw him was in Paris after the War, in company with the conductor Anthony Bernard. But dear Alec Robertson was with us in Bristol, a courteous and civilized gentleman if ever there was one; and also a newcomer to the department, Elizabeth Poston, whose composition *Sweet Suffolk Owl* had endeared her to us all, long before she arrived. She proved to be a most intelligent and agreeable colleague.

It was not too long into 1941, when I was told, via Kenneth Wright on one of his visits to Bristol, that I was to be sent back to London, to look after the music in the newly growing European Service. My knowledge of some French and German doubtless made Management feel I might be a suitable candidate, and I certainly never regretted the transfer! The new job was fascinating in many ways. We had to broadcast to the occupied countries of Europe, and it was thought valuable to send music, even if few were able to listen to it. But, it was necessary to play Chopin for the Poles, and Smetana for the Czechs, and we knew that people did listen, for sometimes word would get back to us. One time, an old friend of Myra Hess, stranded in occupied France, got a message back to say she had been so happy to hear Myra playing and know she was still alive. We were able also to serve the Norwegians and the Greeks and the Yugo-Slavs this way; I had enough money to mount a 40 minute orchestral concert once a week. The man who made this musically possible was the conductor Walter Goehr, who was prepared to mount a weekly concert on one rehearsal, provided he had his chosen and experienced players. Goehr's knowledge of the repertoire and his musical sympathies were very wide, and he did wonderful service for a long time. I had met him first in Light Music, with his "Orchestre Raymonde", a highly competent and versatile body of players, who in fact were the nucleus of the orchestra which played now for the European Service. Goehr proved the ideal man to run a show of this kind, where we could accommodate a range of music from Pezel to Lehar and Kalman, via Bach, Mendelssohn and Mahler. There was no dearth of good soloists either, for the "forbidden" repertoire of Jewish composers. One baritone, engaged to sing Mahler's *Wayfarer's Songs (Lieder eines fahrenden Gesellen)*, was so overcome with emotion at the thought that he might be the first German singer to be allowed again to sing Mahler, that he broke down sobbing in the middle of the performance.

The French and German Services had their own music, and to run it, the Germans had Berthold Goldschmidt, and the French had Francis Chagrin, both of whom became my friends. With Chagrin I felt especially close. He was a most charming man, Rumanian by birth and French by adoption, who became fully integrated into London musical life. With him as the main instigator a group of us formed the Society (originally "Committee") for the Promotion of New Music, which lasted for a great number of years. Associated with us were Matyas Seiber, Benjamin Frankel, and Arnold Goldsbrough.

The French and German Services had more money at their disposal than I; they needed it too, for their responsibilities were greater, especially the French whose programmes included the serial *Babar the Elephant,* and the channels for delivering messages in code to the French Underground. Berthold Goldschmidt helped to keep the German non-Nazi musical flag flying in exile. This was the period when we, the English, insisted on interning those anti-Nazi Germans who had got to our shores. It seemed particularly insular and short-sighted to have people like the composer Franz Reizenstein working as railway clerks, and Norbert Brainin[14] in an internment camp, while for so long that wretch Oswald Mosley[15] was allowed his liberty.

Connected with the European Service, there were two people who were of the greatest help to me in finding material. Joseph Loewenbach, of Prague, is someone I remember with pleasure, affection and regret. Pleasure and affection, because he was so likeable a character, and so devoted to his country's cause. He worked for the Czech government-in-exile, and had come away from Prague, on the last possible train to Vienna in 1938, bringing with him hampers full of Czech music, "just in case". In getting all this safely onto the train, he lost track of his wife, and she was left behind. Joseph spent the whole war listening to the Czech radio, hoping not to hear his wife's name amongst those executed that day. In the end, they were reunited in Prague, and his country's grateful thanks to Joseph was to squander him in the Supraphon factory in a menial position. He was an old-time Liberal, of the Masaryk–Benes school; the new Communist Government had no room for people like him. After the war, when it became possible to travel to Prague again, we got differing reports on Loewenbach, according to the political colour of the English visitors. Those with left-wing sympathies reported that he was "fine; doing a worthwhile job and content with his position". Others, with more liberal standards, described him as depressed and despondent, with nothing to do worthy of his brains or knowledge. He died not too long after the end of the War.

My Polish helper, like Loewenbach, supplied me with his country's music and introduced me to composers like Moniuszko and Jarecki, until then, to me, merely names in a dictionary. He was Mr. Lubinski, a lawyer, and I have forgotten his first name. After the end of the war I lost touch with him; but ten years later I met some of his compatriot composers in their own territory.

It was at this juncture, early in 1942, that I got married for the first time. Marianne Bardas was a German refugee. Her father Willy Bardas had been a concert pianist (and had, I think, met my father many years previously), her mother was a singer, and her slightly older brother Stefan was also a pianist. Marianne herself was a dancer, trained at the Jooss School in Berlin. After Willy Bardas's death, his widow re-married; a Swiss businessman. So she was able to escape from Germany and live, without terror, in Switzerland. But her children, being both German and Jewish, were forced to emigrate. Stefan went to the United States and Marianne came to London. Her mother died before the War ended, and so I never met her, though I did meet and became very fond of Marianne's step-father, Otto Haas.

Early in our marriage, after our two children, Naomi and Nicholas, were born, Marianne made some effort to recover her dance technique, and she did in fact dance in the Glyndebourne production of Gluck's *Orfeo* in 1947. But our marriage was a success only at first. Maybe we had been carried away by the tensions and unrest of war-time; but it seemed that there was insufficient affection to sustain the partnership. In 1957 our marriage broke apart, and I did not see Naomi and Nicholas again for very many years.

Naomi and Nicholas both went into the musical profession; Naomi as a jazz singer and vocal teacher in Munich, and Nicholas as a pianist and music-organizer in San Francisco. We met again in my 88th year (1996), and it was a lovely occasion. I was happy that they found their step-sisters sympathetic human beings, and we all six (Naomi, Nicholas, Margaret, Debbie, my wife Ishbel and myself) attempted, pretty successfully, to bridge the long gap, and begin to establish a good relationship. At the tail-end of my life, that was deeply satisfying.

In early 1943 I was "called up". Some friends, including Vaughan Williams, tried to get my "reserved occupation" prolonged, but to no avail; and I found myself before long in the RAF Band. This was not really very strange. At the start of the war the Musical Director of the RAF saw an opportunity of acquiring something he had long craved, namely a symphony orchestra of his very own. He got his establishment very much increased, and let it be known that he was prepared to accept all the good young string players he could manage to house. In this way he attracted half the strings of the Boyd Neel Orchestra (Boyd Neel himself was a doctor in the Army). Many another freelance violinist and cellist were drawn in, too, and he ended up with a complement of string players to make a war-time conductor's mouth water. He had, into the bargain, the whole Griller Quartet[16] in his orchestra! The wind players were selected with just as much care; he had the Brain brothers, Dennis on horn and Leonard on oboe; Gareth Morris and Edward Walker as flutes; Sandy Jacob on clarinet and Cecil James on bassoon. His second horn was the conductor Norman Del Mar. This was the group I used to be able to book for concerts in the BBC European Service!

The Wing-Commander R.P. O'Donnell would conduct, and the strings were led by David Martin. Behind him would sit Frederick Grinke, Harry Blech, Max Salpeter, Leonard Hirsch, Maurice Loban; violas Max Gilbert and Watson Forbes; cellos James Whitehead and James Harvey Phillips; and James Merrett on double bass. Of these string players, I had been a fellow student at R.C.M. with Jimmy Whitehead and Jim Merrett, and most of the others had been known to me for a long time, Blech and Hirsch since my boyhood in Manchester.

Of the three Canadians, I'd known Grinke and Martin since 1928 when they arrived in London from Winnipeg, along with Zara Nelsova. And I had known the Griller Quartet since my entry into the BBC. So, I was among friends, and once again a performing musician; fourth horn; but inside the services. Like all the other brass players I had to do band fatigues too; marches, funerals, etcetera. On one never-to-be-forgotten occasion the RAF Band found itself at the saluting base opposite Buckingham Palace, for a big parade of all the services. The Wing-Commander had arranged a special signal with his adjutant, so he might be warned when the RAF contingent was approaching, and we could break into the RAF March Past. Unfortunately he was a highly nervous man, and, catching sight of an RAF uniform in the crowd, mistook it for the main contingent, and gave the sign for the March-past to begin. We played it 35 times through before the RAF actually came into view! By that time, I was partly deaf, through standing just in front of the big drum; and I am sure that the Queen (and maybe even the King) knew that something was wrong!

There were few parades of that kind though; the Wing-Commander tried to avoid them if he possibly could. The trouble was that although by Military Band standards he was a veritable Toscanini, by Toscanini's standards he was just a bandmaster. It was a peculiar way to "serve one's country", and I think I had been doing more good in the BBC. But, at the end of the War all these first-rate musicians were still alive and playing, and Wing-Commander O'Donnell had had his orchestra. The only composer before whom he conducted himself with becoming humility was Elgar. With him he really tried hard. Otherwise; well, for instance, he was asked by his concertmaster David Martin (who rarely asked anything, for fear of being shot down) "Tonight, Sir, in the opening of *Borodin II* are you going to beat two or four?" The reply was "That's for you to find out". No wonder we found it hard to take this sort of "service" seriously. Music and service discipline do not mix: either you obey orders or you play Beethoven. You cannot do both, unless you regard the notes on the page as your orders; then, if you play a wrong note, you could find yourself on a charge! This point of view was actually held by one of the band Sergeants! For him on many a Saturday morning, the band would plough through *Reminiscences of Verdi* (or of Puccini, or of...). This was the worst we ever suffered at band Sergeant Sullivan's hands;

the whole of the Finale of Beethoven's *Ninth Symphony*, including all the choral parts scored into the band, all beaten out squarely and relentlessly, four-in-a-bar! (I don't remember *what* he did at "Seid umschlungen"!)

But, there were great compensations, for me at least, in all this. After 13 years I was playing the horn again. Once I'd learned how to handle the heavy Boosey and Hawkes instrument that the RAF were able to issue me, I thoroughly enjoyed being in an orchestra. It had never entered my head that someday I might be one of a quartet of which the first player was Dennis Brain. He was a wonderful and most accomplished horn player, like his father Aubrey[17], but with, I think, an even mellower sound. Dennis's technique was also infallible. I never heard him play a wrong or split note, so it was in fact quite a responsibility to be fourth horn in a group led by him. There is one note in Dvořák's *G major Symphony* which I never played in all the performances we did of that work! Little pianissimo chords in the slow movement; for the fourth horn the note is a written G sharp, that's to say, 2nd and 3rd valves. A finicky note, which offered a deal of resistance, and was apt to "blurt" if it spoke at all. I was so afraid it might come out wrong and spoil the chord, that I never dared to make it sound! The Wing-Commander did not notice; and if Dennis did, he never said anything!

There is another recollection I have of Dvořák *No. 8,* which still causes me to laugh. We were to give a performance of it in a place near London called Staines. Our normal second horn in the orchestra was sick (not Del Mar; if four horns were called for, he played 3rd), so as a substitute the Wing-Commander had detailed Corporal Robinson, who was the regular first horn in the band, but hardly ever did any orchestral work. He had the reputation of being able to play louder than any other living horn player; and anyone who'd ever heard him practising high Cs would believe the tale! Anyway, the Corporal was delighted with the "night out", and played pretty loud from the word go. This caused Dennis Brain to give him a few sidelong glances, but none of them reached Robinson; he was beyond outside influences! The Finale of this Symphony has some very florid places for the quartet of horns, and they're marked "ff" (Very Loud!). Seeing this coming, Corporal Robinson started to increase his volume, and after glancing at him once more, Dennis began to equal him. So of course Norman Del Mar and I had to do likewise. By the end of the piece we were all four purple in the face, and I am sure the audience heard nothing at all but us *horns*! Dennis was furious; but the Corporal was absolutely unaware that he'd caused any sort of débacle; he went home blissfully happy. Such is inno-cence combined with ignorance.

In the latter part of 1944 we were sent to the United States, to help in a war loan drive. While we were abroad, the U.S. First Army Air Force Band was doing the same thing in England; they played all the factories and Stations we had been doing previously. In the States we played on airfields and at camps; we played in Constitution Hall, Washington D.C. and in other fine places. We saw an enormous part of that gigantic country; some of it breathtakingly lovely, and some very exciting. We travelled everywhere by train, so we saw a lot of scenery; and a lot of people too; from Richmond, Virginia to Miami; from New Orleans to Salt Lake City; from Macon, Georgia to San Francisco. Wherever they could, the Americans arranged parties, and we met a great deal of good-will and most generous hospitality: a dance in Greensborough, North Carolina; a Sergeants' Mess party on camp at Macon, Georgia; and a wonderful one we gave ourselves in Sioux Falls, South Dakota, which was the nearest we got to Winnipeg, in Canada. The families of our three Winnipeg string players (Fred Grinke, David Martin and Maurice Loban) came to the hotel in Sioux Falls; it was a heart-warming reunion in which so many of us could share. The warmth was certainly needed, for out of doors was cold and raw, and the camp most unwelcoming. Fred Grinke's father worked for the railways, and I think the whole group got free passes for the 600 mile journey; in North America 600 miles is "not far off"!

Near the end of the tour we were in New York. Yehudi Menuhin and his Australian wife lived there at that time; they invited the strings, and out of courtesy the two pianists, Denis Matthews and myself, and threw a party. It was a wonderful evening; Malcolm Sargent was there, and the celebrated Russian cellist Raya Garbousova, and later on Fritz Kreisler himself came! The violinists were deeply moved, and awed, to find them-selves in the same room with him. Later that night, when I walked down Fifth Avenue with the normally very sober Max Salpeter, he kept hold-ing his right arm out in front of him and saying "D'you see? *This* has shaken hands with *Kreisler*!"

All this sort of jollification did not suit the Wing-Commander at all; he disliked parties, and was very suspicious of his men. When things were "good" we were his music-making buddies, his "boys"; but when he was a bit out of sorts, we were just "airmen" and he was an Officer. Class dies hard.

We should love to have had the chance to play for a really fine conductor; we had the potential of being a first-rate orchestra. Occasionally, on a Saturday morning in Uxbridge, the Wing Commander would turn on one or other member of the orchestra to conduct for a while. He thought it was a bit of a joke, but we often got great enjoyment from these efforts. And one day he called on Harry Blech. For whatever reason, Brahms' *First Symphony* was out on the desks. Harry behaved with the utmost seriousness; for him this was a performance of *Brahms I*; and after the first few bars, so it was for us too. I do not remember another rehearsal that gave us all so much satisfaction. Maybe it was this experience which directed Harry to conducting; he was developing arthritis and finding violin playing increasingly difficult. He made an excellent conductor, and shortly after leaving the RAF he founded the London Mozart Players. It was with great pleasure that some few years later I engaged him, his orchestra, and Menuhin, to broadcast all the Mozart *Violin Concertos*. They were very rewarding musical occasions.

The RAF Orchestra had another American connection. For a while, we joined forces (in the UK) with a big male choir made up of black members of the American Army stationed in England. They made a magnificent sound, and they sang spirituals with beauty and fervour. For our final concert together, we received a visit from that great black singer Roland Hayes, who had at one time been a pupil of Sir George Henschel. The choir regarded this visit as a huge compliment, and were delighted when Hayes sang with them; we too found it touching. The choir was disbanded after a short time; we reckoned it had been too successful.

To revert to New York; 1945 was the year of that nauseating film about Chopin, with Merle Oberon as Georges Sand! I went to see it and got disturbing (disturbing, that is, for my neighbours) fits of giggles when Liszt, visiting M. Pleyel, hears a piano being played, rushes downstairs and finds Chopin sitting there. He has a MS on the music-rack, Liszt sits down next to him on a duet bench, and together they sight-read the *A-flat Polonaise* à quatre mains!! Could anything be more idiotic and falsely sentimental, as well as practically impossible? To cap it all, in the end, given the choice of a handful of Polish soil or Merle Oberon, the silly ass chooses the soil! That should have put me off films about composers for good, but some forty years later I went to see the one supposedly about Mozart; *Amadeus*. It disgusted me. I found it stupid, scurrilous, and also untrue. I still find it hard to understand why it was accepted as viable by so many people. Was it only because of the undeniably splendid playing by the Academy of St. Martin? It is, in my view, indecent that someone (or some people) can make a pile of money out of defamation of the character of one of the world's greatest artists. Certainly, I will never again go to see a film about a famous composer!

I guess we were very lucky to have made two Atlantic crossings by boat in 1944-45 without mishap. Our next trip as musical ambassadors was made by air. The strings and the two pianists were sent to Potsdam, to entertain the staff of the Conference, and, as it turned out, the Principals too. We were placed in a camp among strongly aromatic pine trees, and sent over to Sans-Souci by bus. In Potsdam, directing the traffic, were the most statuesque Russian policewomen. We tried in vain to get them to smile, but they only deepened their solemnity! One evening, we were to play at a dinner given by Mr. Churchill, who was living in what had been Goering's villa. There was a big room, at right angles to the dining room, which had enough space for the orchestra; there was also a grand piano, and sufficient music stands. And there we waited until the guests were assembled; Churchill himself, Stalin, Truman, Molotov, Lord Portal, and many other dignitaries. We watched, entranced, as they downed glass after glass of vodka! The orchestra played many selections from its repertoire; the pianists were not really needed.

Then the big moment arrived: the Three Great Men came into the orchestra's room and stood in a row, backed by all their colleagues. We wondered who would speak first. It was Stalin, who asked if we could play some Borodin (who had been Molotov's uncle). We had no Borodin, but the Wing-Commander said we could play them some Tchaikovsky. So they started on the last movement of the Tchaikovsky

Serenade. I do not think there can ever have been more brilliant or impassioned a performance; it positively glittered! Hardly anyone looked at either the beat or the music. They played "auswendig"; and those members of the band who were politically left-wing (or, as they were called in those days, "fellow-travellers") simply looked at "Uncle Joe" and played to Him. He had not yet fallen from grace! When the movement was over, Stalin made another remark, which was to the effect that that had been very nice, but he supposed Beethoven was in fact the greatest composer. "No, he wasn't" said Mr. Truman, "Mozart was. I'll show you". Stepping to the piano, he pushed Denis Matthews off the bench, and sitting down himself, started to play the opening of the Mozart *A major Sonata, K.331,* the one with variations. It really was fairly creditable. (I should be so good a President of the United States!) We imagined he had to try and 'keep his end up', since he and Molotov were the only ones not in some gorgeous uniform, just plain lounge-suits. After about 16 bars Mr. Churchill turned half sideways and pulled a face at Stalin, a rather rueful grimace. Then they all left, and we hoped for some refreshment; after all, we'd been there for five hours. All they had for 28 of us was one jug of lemonade and one cake. There's the British Army for you!

Shortly after this I was demobilized, and went back to the BBC European Service, but the incentive was no longer the same. The one highlight I remember from the next months was the 70th birthday greeting which we organized for Casals, then living in Prades in the south of France. It was December 1946. We assembled some 70 cellists from all over the British Isles; engaged Barbirolli (himself a cellist) to conduct them, and they played the Prelude from Bach's *Solo Suite in G,* all of them in unison; and then Casals's own *Sardana for 8 cellos.* It was indeed a gorgeous sound, and we learned that Casals had been pleased. The announcer, a tall good-looking Spaniard named Juan Manye, was very much moved at the thought of actually addressing Casals (in Catalan, I think), and could hardly speak for emotion.

≡VIII≡
The BBC
The Third Programme Years

I THINK THAT IT WAS IN 1947 that I was moved back to Head Office. Including the interval in the RAF it was six years since I had been sent to the European Service, and I was quite glad to move, although I had made some good and lasting friendships in Bush House. During the time I was there I had two assistants; for a while my old friend the composer John Greenwood (office-work did not suit him at all!); and later another distinguished composer, Lennox Berkeley. While I was away in the Forces my deputy was Steuart (later Sir Steuart) Wilson, who became the next BBC Head of Music. I believe Elizabeth Poston did the job for a while too.

I was brought back to be something called "Music Programme Organiser". It was a dogsbody of a job, but one which took every ounce of one's patience and ingenuity. A simple description would be to say that the job was to see that the wishes and plans of the Programme Builders, as laid out on paper, came to actual fruition in the studio. Not as simple as it sounds, as I found to my cost. One of the more amusing headaches which I remember, was the time when one of my newer colleagues, still rather unused to process, stated on paper that on such and such a date there would be, in the then-new Third Programme, a performance of a big choral work, using the BBC Symphony Orchestra, the BBC Chorus, Sir Adrian Boult and some solo singers; the whole to take place in Westminster Cathedral! The date of the performance was a day on which the Orchestra was detailed to the Home Service; it turned out that no-one had been approached except the Cardinal Archbishop of

Westminster; not even Sir Adrian! That took some sorting out. That was the kind of problem with which one's time was apt to be filled, as MPO. The BBC was great on initials for positions. I was referred to on documents, not by name, but as "MPO"; my colleague who organized music for the Third Programme (by far the most interesting and prestigious job inside the Music department) was known as "TPMO"; so that even if the person changed, the job didn't. It did make for some administrative clarity; a much-needed ingredient in our work!

The position of MPO brought a few unexpected benefits. In 1947 I was sent to Brussels, representing the department at some European Radio Conference[18]. During that year and the next I was sent off to Zürich and to Hamburg; and so I met the conductors Paul Sacher and Hans Schmidt-Isserstedt; and oversaw the making of special recordings which the BBC were buying. Thus also, I made the acquaintance of Frank Martin's music, and gained a very good idea of the qualities of both aforementioned conductors. Later on in my career I was able to put this to good use; for the time being, it was great just to watch these excellent musicians and their orchestras in action, and to enjoy their first-class music-making.

It was quite disarming, in Hamburg, to find that indeed the Nazis' ridiculous embargo on "Jewish Art" meant that for this young NWDR Orchestra[19] Mendelssohn's *Midsummer Night's Dream Overture* was a new work! In Hamburg too, the young first oboist came up to me to ask if Leon Goossens was still alive. His relief at finding that Goossens was still playing was quite touching. As far as the conductors were concerned, both Sacher and Schmidt-Issertsedt did great work for the BBC in future years; the German Schmidt-Isserstedt, too young to have been indoctrinated, became a regular visitor, while the Swiss Sacher conducted the first performance (in the Third Programme) of Stravinsky's *Rake's Progress*. This was, in fact, its première in England; the Edinburgh Festival having lost out to the BBC. Sacher also conducted at Glyndebourne.

An MPO has only a vicarious connection with actual music-making: oils the wheels, so to speak, for others. But I watched these wheels going round with enormous interest. One of those "wheels" was the one which operated the Third Programme's affairs. We had all sensed a change of some sort was due; in 1950 it came about, and I was put in charge of the

Third Programme's music. This was a year of many changes in the BBC, for Sir Adrian Boult retired as Conductor of the Symphony Orchestra (much against his will) and was succeeded by Sir Malcolm Sargent; and the new Head of Music was my close friend Herbert Murrill. He, incidentally, had only another two years to live. He died of cancer in 1952, a very sad loss to me, as well as to the profession and the BBC.

Around this same time, late 1949 I think, I began to translate Bach's *Art of Fugue* for a small chamber ensemble. Two of my friends of many years, the flautist John Francis and his wife, harpsichordist Millicent Silver, had requested me to do this. They ran the group called the London Harpsichord Ensemble and were to give a row of concerts at the Edinburgh Festival of 1950. It was the bicentenary of Bach's death, and they wanted to include *Art of Fugue*. The performance duly took place, and was a success. I was quite delighted; as I have been with subsequent performances in London (Boyd Neel), Montreal (Alexander Brott), Halifax (Georg Tintner), and Winnipeg (William Baerg and Bramwell Tovey).

I spent four years as TPMO, and they were the most productive years of my BBC service. The Third Programme had been started in 1946 as a service for the listener who switched on what he wanted to hear, as distinct from switching off what he didn't like. In principle there was no time limit to the length of an individual item, so it would be possible to broadcast a complete opera, or a complete play by Shakespeare or Euripides, or to conduct a full-length enquiry or discussion. It would be possible to serialize programmes in such a way as to accommodate *all* the Beethoven *String Quartets*, or the whole of the *Well-Tempered Klavier*. There would be a place for the most outré of contemporary music, or the most recondite of ancient music; as also there would be room for talks and lectures addressed to the most interested and informed or inquisitive audiences. The whole idea of the Third Programme was one of the most courageous and imaginative occurrences in the whole story of European broadcasting; and to me this new job was an invitation to an organizational heaven. I had £3,000 a week to administer, a very civilized Controller of Third Programme to satisfy, and the obligation to keep within my budget. An opera could only take place at carefully calculated intervals, and money could not be squandered, but there was enough to be able to satisfy almost any taste.

I had to produce a three-monthly plan, as did my opposite number in Home Service. It was up to us to make the wisest use we could of the abilities and known specialties of our colleagues. I had now won the forum for "contemporary music", a genus of which I had never been enamoured. I was leery of doctrinaire approaches to the act and technique of composition. In order to appeal to my interest or sympathy (or delight), a work did not have to be written in any one preordained style: I looked for a convincing communication, one which made its logic apparent to my ears, not my eyes. I could aurally follow a fugal argument by Bach (or by Honegger), but if that argument were based on an atonal "row" of 12 notes and I couldn't follow it with my ears, but would need a score to observe when there were inversions, canons, stretti, and so on, thus listening to music with my eyes, I failed to recognize it as music, and was apt to think its author might have been better employed in painting or sculpting. I still feel that way!

Nevertheless, there was in Third Programme an opportunity for the most iconoclastic of composers to find a buyer. Similarly there was also an opportunity to make up for one's fairly certain ignorance of the bulk of, say, Haydn's music. The possibilities seemed, and were, infinite. I had a very fine second-in-command in Robert Simpson, who had joined the department a short time previously. There had, however, been enough time for me to be able to assess not only his enterprise and interest, but also (and more importantly) the depth of his musical judgement. He was a composer himself, who is as non-doctrinaire as I suppose it is possible to be and still retain a very firm personal point of view. He is reputed once to have said that he would not be found dead with a tone-row in his pocket. Nor would I! That did not prevent the works of the dodecaphonists from being heard on Third Programme, but not to the exclusion of other types of contemporary music. Indeed, it was under my aegis that we mounted a series of commemorative programmes on Arnold Schoenberg, who had died in 1951. I was roundly taken to task by Erwin Stein (in, of all places, the Times Bookshop!) for having engaged a non-Schoenbergian, namely Michael Tippett, to host the series, rather than a disciple. Erwin Stein was one of the directors of Boosey & Hawkes, a pupil of Schoenberg's, and definitely a disciple! But, it was precisely the imbalance of discipleship that I had wished to avoid; and thanks to Michael Tippett's moderation and intelligence, succeeded in doing.

Another series which afforded me a great deal of satisfaction and pleasure was a set of broadcasts on the *Origins of Christian Chant* which was prepared for us by Professor Egon Wellesz. It turned out to be, as I had hoped, a most scholarly and serious undertaking, which stretched our resources quite considerably. Dr. Wellesz seemed to have pupils who dealt in the sort of scholarship needed for these programmes all over Europe and the Near East. So, we collected recordings for him from Israel, and also the Yemen (via Dr. Edith Gerson-Kiwi in Jeruslaem), Morocco and Vienna. I thought that this kind of programming was fulfilling the Third Programme's mandate quite properly. I have already mentioned *Rake's Progress* which happened in my time, as also did the first English performances of Messaien's *Turangalila Symphony* under Walter Goehr, and Dallapiccola's *Il Prigioniero* under Hermann Scherchen. It was amusing, in a way, that without any intention of so being, I became the BBC's "thermometer" for Contemporary Music. I was sent to ISCM[20] Festivals in Frankfurt, Salzburg, Haifa, Paris, Donaueschingen, and finally Warsaw. These were all interesting; far more so for the people I met than for the music I heard! The atonal bug had bitten everybody, regardless of geography, so that there was hardly any noticeable difference between a work written in Italy and one written in Argentina or Norway. I found this all rather boring. There were few oases; it seemed to me that "inspiration" (if it is still a reality) was running out, everywhere. That is, until I reached Warsaw in 1956 and made my first acquaintance with the music of Lutoslawski and Bacewicz; and, three years later, Penderecki.

In spite of my feelings about the majority of the contemporary music, I was deeply grateful to the BBC for enabling me to see so much of Europe. The foreign trips included two to Italy to vote in the Prix Italia: and certainly that exercise introduced me to one or two composers whom I might otherwise not have met; Petrassi, Mario Zafred and his poet Stefano Terra, and Eugene Bozza.

Altogether, at the BBC, what I found most gratifying and attractive was the kind of fellowship which grew up among radio people. I guess this is not a surprising thing to have happened, but it struck me afresh each new place that I visited; one met "one's own kind". Whether they worked for a Communist Government or a less restrictive authority seemed to make little difference. So, for instance, at one festival in Paris, I met two men from the East German Radio, and was able to arrange with them an exchange broadcast to take place later, between the choirs of King's College Cambridge and the Thomaskirche in Leipzig (Bach's church), with an all-Bach programme. It did happen, and I thought Cambridge won! But I was told off by Management for having dared to talk to Communists without permission!

The Italian Radio (RAI) paid the BBC a fine compliment by naming its "highbrow" network "Terzo Programma" and I remember with pleasure Mario Labroca and Alberto Mantelli, and their excellent conductor in Turin, Mario Rossi. From Brussels there were the two stalwarts Tellier and Collaer; and in Paris, Paul Gilson. The very likeable Hermann Leeb worked in the Swiss Radio, Zürich. He was a good lutenist, and a sensitive and civilized person; I enjoyed his company greatly. In Israel there was the remarkable Karel Salomon, with a second-in-command who rejoiced in the name Petrushka! And there, too, were Peter Gradenwitz and Frank Pelleg, and the composer Josef Tal, in whom I found a kindred spirit. Dr. Edith Gerson-Kiwi lived there also; Matyas Seiber and I spent a most pleasant evening with her, when we couldn't stand Milhaud's *David* any longer! (I do not find it wrong to admit to boredom; not everything written by a composer with a good reputation is going to be first-class. It is not the case with Vivaldi either!) I recall Hans Rutz of Rot-Weiss-Rot in Salzburg, and in Copenhagen the flautist Johan Bentzon, who, though not employed by the Danish Radio, was found to be there when any contemporary music was in question. Alas, I cannot remember the name of the very hospitable Head of Music there, who regaled me with rather a lot of schnapps (Aquavit) and a good lunch, around 3 o'clock in the afternoon. All in all, the network of radio people was far-reaching, and always friendly.

This is all being written some 40 years later than it actually happened, but my most vivid memories of contacts I made with another radio organization come from 1956. In that year Poland arranged its first contemporary festival since 1939. The war had intervened, and between the Nazis and the Russians, virtually no music by composers living in the West had been heard. The Festival was an undertaking requiring some courage to proceed with, for Russian troops were within a few miles of Warsaw still, and Russian "supervision" if not actual interference, was expected. In the result it was all allowed to take place, though we were told that the Russians were becoming a little restive; the Festival was being too much a success!

Visiting orchestras came from Moscow, Bucharest, and Vienna. Music by hitherto proscribed composers was being heard, and applauded to the echo. Alfred Brendel played the Schoenberg *Piano Concerto*, and it was encored! He had to repeat part of it! Berg's *Lyric Suite* was played by the Parrenin String Quartet; Stravinsky's *Ebony Concerto* was heard for the first time in Poland; and many other works too, which by then were normal in Western Europe. There were also some admirable works by Polish composers, brand new to the few Western listeners who had been invited. The invités numbered only six: Peter Heyworth, music critic of the London Observer; a young Norwegian composer, Poul Rovsing-Olson; an American writer on music from Munich (I think it was Paul Moores); myself representing the BBC; and Nadia Boulanger from Paris, with her companion Estelle de Manziarly. Nadia Boulanger had been the teacher of almost every Polish composer of the previous generation, and she was the Queen of the Festival. Even the gentleman representing the USSR Radio was pushed slightly to one side in the big concert hall, to let Madame sit in the centre of the front row of the balcony! Madame had a car permanently at her disposal, and she was clearly the centre of all interest. The lecture she gave in the Salle Chopin was overflowing, and well worth attending too, if only to see what a consummate actress she was. Her address appeared impromptu; she even pretended to be surprised that she was expected to speak! But she spoke extremely well, and ended by "just happening to have with her" a copy of the then quite new *Canticum Sacrum* of Stravinsky, which she proceeded to demonstrate. She ended with the marvelous remark, "Every time 'Le Maître' writes another work, people say 'this time he really has gone mad', but after a little while they see that he was right. Le Maître is always right!" I enjoyed this enormously; I had repaired the stupid omission of my Paris student months, and had come to know Madame at the BBC; and had come also to admire and respect her. The Polish composers obviously worshipped her!

Besides making the acquaintance of some of the Polish composers in Warsaw, I also got to know the very knowledgeable and enterprising members of Radio Polskie's Music Department. I made particular friends with their Head of Music, Roman Jasinski, and with his assistant, Bachner. There was also Jan Krenz the conductor, and the man I'd known in London as the conductor of the Polish Army Choir, Kolaczkowski. Although it was never said in so many words, I got the impression that Radio Polskie was the big force behind the Festival. It was successful enough to warrant a repeat, and I went again in 1959, when there were far more Westerners.

At the 1956 Festival each of us visitors was given a "guide". In my case it was a young and impoverished university student, whose job it was to see that I got where I wanted to go, and got home safe too. There was a party after one of the orchestral concerts; I think it was after the Rumanian orchestra, whose violin section must all have been Gypsies! I have never before heard such fat luscious tone. At this party I got to speak with Lutoslawski. I found him easy to get on with, well-informed, civilized and altogether charming. We talked so long that my young guide thought he'd better break things up, and get me back to the hotel. I told him that I was old enough to find my own way back if I had to, and that I was *too* old to be told when it was time to go! But I felt a bit sorry for him, since it was clear he had to hang around; I guess he had to make a report when he finally got me safely back indoors.

The concert performance which affected me the most was the visiting Russian orchestra's *Tchaikovsky No. 5*, conducted by a man called Konstantin Ivanov. That piece is surely a war horse if ever there was one, but in their hands it became as new; fresh, impressive, beautiful, and in the finale, absolutely electrifying. The last entry of the big tune was like a national anthem; one wanted to stand to attention. I was very deeply moved, and do not really want to hear the *Symphony* again, for that impression to be tampered with. It was the final answer to the people who maul the symphony about, and make it cheap, mawkish and saccharine. *Why* will performers either emasculate or exaggerate both Tchaikovsky and Chopin, and rob them of their manhood, their humanity, and turn them into cheap magazine pin-ups?

The 1956 Warsaw Festival lasted about a week, by which time there were rumours (unfounded) that the Russian troops were encircling the city again. We were, I know, all glad to board a KLM plane and get out of the east. But I came away with very cordial feelings towards the country where Chopin is a national hero; and too, with warmer feelings towards my one-time Polish colleague at Bush House, Czeslaw Halski.

The Third Programme had other things besides contemporary music to offer, too; such as many broadcasts by that wonderful ensemble the Amadeus Quartet. All four of them became very dear friends of mine. We broadcast the musical partnership of violinist Max Rostal, the Amadeus' teacher, and pianist Franz Osborn; and visits from conductors like Bruno Walter, Otto Klemperer, Klecki, Horenstein, the marvelous Pierre Monteux, and Rafael Kubelik. And one conductor whom I will never forget, Georges Enesco, whose Bach *B minor Mass* made so lasting an impression on all of us who were present. It was one of the last occasions on which Kathleen Ferrier sang for us, and her presence and her singing made of the *Mass* a thing of almost unbearable emotional intensity. Enesco was a devoted conductor, respected by everyone, and by the time the *Agnus Dei* was reached we were all affected. I have never before (or since) seen the principal cellist of a famous orchestra playing with tears running down his cheeks. Alas, neither he (James Whitehead) nor Kathleen nor Enesco are with us any longer; nor Peter Pears who was the tenor in the performance. He was also much moved by Kathleen's singing that day, though they must have worked together many times before. I do not suppose that Bach has ever been served with greater humility or love, or greater majesty, than in that performance.

Another occasion which engendered much emotion, though not at all as upsetting as the *B minor Mass*, was the first time David Oistrakh came to England. Following its usual behaviour, the Soviet Embassy one day informed the BBC (or, more probably, the Government) that, very soon, a group of Russian artists would be visiting England, and they required broadcast space for them. The group would be headed by David Oistrakh, the great violinist, of whom we had heard glittering reports. The short notice we received was also according to custom. The visit was to be in three weeks' time, and our programmes were usually complete

at least six weeks in advance, if not more! So we tore apart the plans for
that period, found a space in Third Programme, an orchestra; the Royal
Philharmonic was available but not its conductor, Beecham, so it would
be Sir Malcolm Sargent to conduct. And Oistrakh would play? *The
Tchaikovsky,* of course. Well, the group of artists duly arrived (I believe
the then quite young Emil Gilels was a member of it). Their entry into
the Maida Vale Studios was accompanied by a throng of well-wishers
from the Society for Cultural Relations with the U.S.S.R. But when it
came to Oistrakh's day, he was accompanied only by one little lady interpreter (he had as yet no English) and his violin case. The interpreter was
not needed, for a member of the orchestra spoke Russian, and the
rehearsal went ahead.

Everything went smoothly, there was no difficulty of any kind; and
like all great artists, Oistrakh was no trouble either. In the evening the
excitement was high. A small studio audience was permitted. Alfredo
Campoli had phoned and actually asked permission to come to the studio; we'd have let him in if he had just turned up! Even Sir Malcolm was
nervous. Most unusual for him to show it, but when he put his hand on
my shoulder, just before entering the studio, it was shaking! The performance was captivating, and Oistrakh showed himself to be the consummate fiddler we'd heard about; quite devoid of show-off or bombast. At
the end of the *Concerto* everyone in the studio applauded, including the
members of the orchestra. In fact, the strings would not leave! They got
up from their chairs and moved across the floor, so that they ended by
encircling Oistrakh, while still clapping. After a moment or two he
understood, and played the Bach *Chaconne,* just for them alone. A lovely
gesture, and one of which the news must have gone quickly round the
profession, for from that moment Mr. Oistrakh was not only "persona
grata" to all musicians, but greatly welcome to all London, as was his
pianist Vladimir Yampolsky when the next visit occurred (By that time
both men had acquired some English). Oistrakh's playing seemed to me
the acme of non-flamboyant classical perfection. Every bar was a joy to
hear and to watch.

Another Russian experience was just after the war, when Shostako-
vich's recently completed *Seventh "Leningrad" Symphony* was finally
released for performance abroad. The BBC invited the Soviet Ambassa-

dor, Ivan Maisky and his wife to a studio performance, and gave a huge party in the Maida Vale Studios. It may have been on Stalin's official birthday (December 21) in whichever year, I simply do not remember. Nor can I remember which orchestra played, nor who conducted! I can only remember being, as they say in Lancashire, "proper moithered" by all the protocol and social arrangements which had to be attended to. I fear I found the *Symphony* rather boring; and I didn't even get to meet Maisky!

Of course, there were other occurrences which occasioned laughter rather than strain. There was the time when the LSO's piccolo player asked that highly explosive American conductor Bernard Herrmann whether he was expected to play some notes which he found pencilled into his part. "Well, what d'you want" shouted Herrmann, "*neon lights?*" And, at a Monteux rehearsal: Monteux was the most courteous of conductors, enormously respected by everyone. (I think he carried with him the aura of the famous première of *Le Sacre du Printemps*.) During a passage where the three trombones had many bars empty, the first player had a newspaper open on his desk. Monteux noticed this and stopped the orchestra; during the ensuing silence the trombonist, realizing that something was happening, looked up, to find Monteux gazing straight at him. Monteux said "Good news, hein?" with that inimitable rise in his voice. The newspaper disappeared immediately, and no more was said, nor needed to be!

During the course of my BBC years I must have met almost every broadcasting artist outside the realms of opera, and it struck me most forcibly that the greater the man or woman, the easier they were to deal with. The really great do not throw tantrums! Of course, it is only natural to do whatever you can to make a Myra Hess or a Sandro Materassi or an André Navarra comfortable and at ease, but on their side they are not apt to make a fuss. They tell you what they may need or want, and you give it them if you possibly can. How else would one behave? I "looked after" many people in the studio; Bruno Walter himself, Monteux, Kubelik, Sacher, Klemperer (of whom I was secretly afraid), Solomon, Curzon, Hess, Menuhin; never, never did I have trouble caused by one of *them*. True, there was the time when Myra Hess fell foul of Hermann Scherchen, but he had been inexcusably rude to her in her own home.

I'll certainly not forget the frigid atmosphere at rehearsal next day, with me sitting at her side in case of "trouble", and communication between soloist and conductor being channeled through the concertmaster!

I had had a very effective introduction into the ways of the great, at the École Normale, as a student. Cortot was invariably courteous, and so was Casals; he was able to be courteous and kindly and most demanding all at the same time. In all probability, Casals was the greatest musician I have ever met (since I didn't meet Rachmaninov). To hear Casals put a frightened student at his or her ease was a lesson in manners. To the terribly nervous American girl at her first encounter with him, whose bowing arm was too quivering with nerves to be kept still enough to play a note, he simply said, with a disarming smile "Yes, my dear, the cello is a very difficult instrument, isn't it?" The atmosphere was cleared, the fear left her, and she could play. So much for the people who shout at their students or their orchestra! It seems to me that only the second-rate need to shout and storm. I never knew if there was some excuse for Toscanini; I only know that when he was given good, adequate playing, he didn't do it. In 1935 he came to London and conducted the BBC Symphony Orchestra. After a concert in which the main work had been the *E minor Symphony* of Brahms, I met the orchestra's Scottish principal flute. We were in a little musicians' club near the Queen's Hall, and Mr. Murchie (who knew me from the R.C.M. where he taught) leaned over and observed, with tremendous solemnity "My boy; I've been playing the flute for forty years, and tonight is the first time I've ever played the solo in *Brahms 4* the way I've always wanted to play it." That is wonderful; the final and absolute compliment to a conductor. I recalled that comment on any occasion when I heard an orchestra or a player being shouted at.

Singers have a bad reputation for fussing, yet perhaps I was simply fortunate; I didn't meet those of whom I needed subsequently to be afraid. It is true that in recital and orchestral work one is not up against the sort of difficulties which one can meet in opera, and I do remember that in the studio-operas with which I came into actual contact (*Rake's Progress* with Sacher, and *Pelléas* with Inghelbrecht), there were problems; though not of the conductors' making. The problems were usually cases of singers' excessive temperament, and in-fighting, and my dear colleague

David Harris, the Opera Manager had to deal with such things if they occurred! Mostly they were pretty infrequent, since people didn't like to offend the BBC.

When I was very new at the BBC I was one day hauled out of the office and asked to go home and practise; Claire Croiza was coming over and she was due to give a recital of Debussy and Roussel. Our chief accompanist, Ernest Lush, was sick, and so I was to play for her; on four days' notice! I was somewhat in awe of this lady, whom I'd never heard, but of whose reputation I was aware, through Marya Freund in Paris (Helen Henschel's cousin). Most of the songs were new to me; certainly the Roussel were; but Croiza was a superlative artist, and her way of singing made each song absolutely clear. There was never any doubt, so it was all plain sailing. I found the same thing with violinists Campoli and Erich Gruenberg[21], when they came to Winnipeg many years later and we did joint recitals at the University of Manitoba. And it had been thus with Ivor Novello too. It is not the great who make trouble!

Well, it is rarely the great who make trouble... I did once have trouble with Sir Thomas Beecham; not too difficult a thing to attain. The Third Programme Controller asked me for a special concert for Christmas week, and there was enough extra money to buy an orchestra. What could be a nicer present for the musical public than an hour or two of Sir Thomas and his Royal Philharmonic Orchestra? So a booking went out, and a request to Sir Thomas to propose his programme. One didn't deal with Beecham direct, but through an intermediary. It took a very long time for anything to happen, but finally a programme suggestion was forthcoming, and to my great surprise it contained a manuscript piece by a quite unknown member of his second violin section. The BBC did not accept MS works without first vetting them. There existed a formal Reading Panel for this purpose, though its advice was often hotly disputed, and equally often proved wrong. In this case, there was no time to invoke such a procedure, and I thought it would arouse a storm if I were to suggest it to Sir Thomas. So I told the intermediary that I was not allowed to programme an MS work without having seen it, and asked for the score to be sent to me. There was more delay, and at first a refusal to send the music. In the end, however, it did arrive, and one look at it was enough for me to recognize a bit of film music; maybe background for a battle scene, for there were a *lot* of trumpet calls over a drone bass (After all, it was not very long since I had been producing just such scores!). I refused to have it in our concert; it was certainly not worthy of a place in the Third Programme's Christmas Concert. I was told that Sir Thomas had promised the young composer a performance. I suppose he thought the BBC was the right place to do it because they would be paying! The tug-of-war went on. Neither side gave in, and in the end I cancelled the booking and we did something else for Christmas. Later I found out that the piece was indeed from a film score which Sir Thomas had accepted sight unseen. I also heard that he had complained to our Director General that he had been thwarted by "some fellow called Isaacs"; which was most impolite of him, since he knew me quite well! But that was Sir Thomas; and he was almost always forgiven. After all, he was a superb conductor, and in almost everything, a law unto himself. When he approached the conductor's podium to begin a concert, the first item sounded as if it were entitled "God Save Sir Thomas!"[22] I have often wondered whether I am the only person ever to have cancelled a booking for Beecham.

The business of arranging orchestral programmes could be entertaining; or troublesome, according to whom you were dealing with. Sir Adrian was plain sailing; he regarded his position as the BBC's Chief Conductor as being one of a purveyor. He would conduct what you asked him to... and complain afterwards if he hadn't liked it! With visiting conductors, either British or foreign, discussions often went on for quite a while; programmes had to be fitted into a long-term scheme. We did not like near repeats of large works; and again, programme content had to balance as between Home Service and Third Programme. The Symphony Orchestra served both wave-lengths, of course, and its very full working week included two concerts each for both Services. This also meant that my opposite number, the Home Service Music Organiser and I had to be well agreed about how much duplication between Services we wanted or needed. The colleague in question, Peter Crossley-Holland, and I saw eye to eye about a good many things. He had joined the BBC in 1948 and we had become close friends; certainly close enough to be able to design a 13 week series of programmes without coming to blows.

When Sir Malcolm Sargent became Chief Conductor in 1950, there needed to be a three-monthly joint "démarche". Peter and I would carefully construct our plans, to contain as many duplications as seemed advisable, to include novelties for Third Programme, and suitable soloists for both Services. We would then make a date to visit Sir Malcolm, together, at his apartment in Albert Hall Mansions; and would hope to win as many tricks as we could. Building a season with Sargent was like a game of bridge, or poker! He would have works which *he* wanted to include, and he was quite likely not to like our suggestions. Indeed, once we suggested a symphony by a somewhat less familiar French composer, and he turned it down out of hand. Since I was the ex-pupil, I rang him the next day and asked him whether I might at least send him the score to look at; if he didn't like it then, there was an end of the matter. Sargent agreed, and liked the symphony very much when he saw it; when the time came, he gave two admirable performances of it. At our next departmental meeting, he looked brightly round the table and exclaimed "Now wasn't that a good idea of mine to do X's 4th Symphony?" Peter and I glanced at each other and winked. And, just as with Beecham, I always could forgive Sargent. I could never forget that wonderful Tchaikovsky of 1929 that we did together; and anyway there was something lovable about him, in spite of his arrogance.

The BBC Music Department in London was a very "in-growing" assemblage of different characters, and it is surprising how well (on the whole) it worked. I remember most of my colleagues there with affection, and the inevitable storms which blew up were usually weathered without too much difficulty. Some departmental institutions, such as the bi-weekly "Artists' Committee" and weekly auditions, were chores which had to be coped with. Even there, there were compensations. One of the functions of the Artists' Committee was to review previously-held auditions, and consider the reports from them. At one meeting, the non-staff person present (we always had one non-staff involved in auditions, to see that fair play prevailed) was that wonderful old lady, Dame Agnes Nicholls[23]. As the reports were read out, we reached those on a particularly ineffective soprano, whose performance we easily recalled. Auditions were always held anonymously, and unseen too. "Oh dear" said Dame Agnes, "was that a woman? I thought it was a baby!"

One piano audition I remember especially clearly. On a small and bad piano, someone had given us a magnificent performance of Ravel's *Ondine*. At the next meeting we discovered it had been the splendid American pianist Abbey Simon. In subsequent years, his playing gave me untold pleasure. He is a musician of real stature; produces a gorgeous sound and never "gets through the tone". I think Prokofiev must have known about Abbey by clairvoyance; his *Toccata* could have been written specifically for Abbey; always a tremendously exciting performance.

And I remember when, at a visitors' audition, a soprano sang well, really well; but when she turned to spirituals it was even more supremely beautiful. We all instinctively put down our pencils and just listened. That was Betty Allen, who properly made a big name for herself.

The BBC's politics spread all over the British Isles. There were the various Regional Offices, and each region had its list of available artists and ensembles. In five of the regions there were BBC Orchestras; in addition there was the Hallé Orchestra in Manchester, the Scottish National in Glasgow, the City of Birmingham, and Bournemouth had its Orchestra too. The pattern of broadcasting was quite complicated if any attempt were made to have the country fairly represented. I think we were reasonably successful. Our regional colleagues visited London every so often, and we used to be glad to pay visits too, and get to know our regional counterparts. For me, as a Mancunian, it was always a special pleasure to visit Manchester; my parents were still there, though my father died in 1953.

The year before that my friend Herbert Murrill had died, and Maurice Johnstone, the current Head of Music for the North Region, was brought to London to succeed him as Head of Music. In 1954 he switched over Peter Crossley-Holland and myself; Peter became "TPMO" and I, "HSMO". It was a sensible thing to do, though I didn't think so at the time. But four years is really quite enough for any one person to cope with that Third Programme job; you have used up most of your available ideas in that space of time.

≡IX≡

Canadian Federation of Music Festivals

Last Years at the BBC

ND NOW I COME to an occurrence which eventually altered my life again. I had been looking for some non-BBC occupation, as a means of finding new perspectives; a species of refreshment. The composer and publisher Maurice Jacobson (of Curwen's) suggested that I might try adjudicating at Music Festivals. After a few preliminary tries, I was offered the Canadian tour. In those days, the Canadian Federation of Music Festivals brought over each year a team of four people from the UK to cover the whole of Canada, from Halifax to Vancouver, not including Quebec[24]. Jacobson himself, along with many other well-known musicians from around the country, had done the tour and told me I would enjoy it, and, he thought, do a good job. My name was given, I was accepted, and so in 1953 I obtained a leave of absence from the BBC and prepared to revisit Canada after 21 years.

There are people who believe very firmly in the value and advantages of the Festival movement; and there are those whose enthusiasm is tempered with some misgivings about the lasting qualities of the advice and assessments which are to be found there. But for me, in 1953, it was a new world and a fascinating one. One's advice was so eagerly sought, even if it were critical. And I was treated so very well and so generously (so were we all) that I failed to realize that the timing of classes was not always carefully enough done. But, in one town after another, I heard music-making of all kinds, by all ages, and not only on my own instrument. The evening sessions were usually built to attract an audience of parents, relatives, and interested townsfolk. Life was less sophisticated then, and less crammed with TV, so that, in fact, the audiences were mostly large and enthusiastic. One had, therefore, a ready public for what one hoped were timely and reasonably light-hearted remarks. Some of us were better at that part of the proceedings than others. I shall never forget the horror with which three of us heard our fourth colleague, who had clearly had much too good a supper, deliver a homily on the virtues of the Church of England, in which he was an organist back home. He compared it rather too favourably to the Roman Catholic Church. He had just been listening to an excellent choir from a Catholic Seminary, and had quite suitably praised its work; but he got carried away into very dangerous and inappropriate territory. That sort of thing was no part of our job, however much one might have had to drink!

One of my fellow adjudicators in 1953 was a very well-known English baritone, whom I had not previously met, though I surely knew his name. This was Gordon Clinton, with whom I developed a dear friendship. At first, we spent some time, aboard the *Queen Mary*, circling round each other, each discovering what breed of musician the other was. What we found suited both of us, and the ensuing tour proved, on a personal basis, extremely pleasing.

Our Festival duties began on the east coast, in Halifax, and then on to Saint John, New Brunswick. I had a very vague recollection of Halifax, for it was the port at which we had embarked to come back to Liverpool in 1932. But now it seemed a quite new place. The experiences we were having were quite new too; including our first Nova Scotia lobster dinner (vast, messy, and delicious) in the home of one of the ladies who ran the Festival, Elsie MacAloney. (Her portrait now hangs in the Music Department of Dalhousie University.) The dinner was wonderful, and Mrs. MacAloney a dynamo of energy and a fountain of goodwill!

Returning to my colleague Gordon Clinton, I found him a singer after my own heart. He sang well and he had a fine, beautiful voice; but with him the music came first and his glory second. Wherever we went, singing contestants were given a true basic account of their responsibilities to Haydn, Schubert, Vaughan Williams, or the operatic composers. This relationship was exactly what I tried to point out to the pianists, and in Clinton's attitude I found confirmation of my own. Some years later, in England, he and I did some recitals together, and he was a joy to work with; the same kind of pleasure I had experienced with another baritone, Henry Cummings. The male singer's repertoire contains so very many fine English songs. When Gordon found a good singer he was full of praise and encouragement, and could sometimes be moved by a student's performance. It was at Stratford we heard the then 18 year old John Boyden give so beautiful a performance of Vaughan Williams's *Silent Noon* that we were both moved to actual tears. That didn't happen very often, but we did hear some excellent playing and singing. What was lacking in almost every part of the country was chamber music; though in Halifax we found an eager and accomplished madrigal group, directed by a local bank manager, and we joined them one evening, for fun.

The group of judges from England was asked to hear mainly the senior contestants; to hear everyone would have taken far too long. So, Canadian adjudicators were co-opted, and thus I first met such people as Charles Peaker, Gladys Whitehead, Martin Boundy, and many, many others. The whole Festival movement was to a large extent supported by the Kiwanis, a men's service club which has, as one of its raisons d'être, the helping of under-privileged children. The argument for Festival support ran thus: if these musical children do not have a proper outlet for their talents, they will become under-privileged. So the "outlet" received very strong support, and in some cities we were held responsible to the Kiwanis. They attended and manned every session, and took us along to Club luncheons at which we usually had to speak (and drink the Queen's health in water, which seemed to us to be lèse majesté!). This was the case in Toronto and in most of the Ontario Festivals we visited; but the centre, from which the engagement of adjudicators emanated, and whence the general directions seemed to be issued, was Winnipeg. There, indeed, the Festival lasted for two full weeks, as it did in Toronto[25] and Vancouver, but there was no service club involved. The whole Canadian Festival movement was really run by three men, representing the Men's Music Club of Winnipeg, an organization which was behind a great deal of Winnipeg's musical life. Richard Cooke, Reginald Hugo and James Seaton were collectively known as the "Three Musketeers", and for years they did a tremendous job of motivating and supporting the Festival across Canada; and most of all in their own city. They have alas, all three passed on now, but the impression they left with any and every adjudicator coming out from England was indelible. For all of us, over so many years, the Winnipeg Festival meant the "Three Musketeers". Richard Cooke and his whole family became very close friends of ours when we settled in Winnipeg in 1963, and that closeness has even grown since his death.

Further west we met the service clubs again; their involvement did not decrease, only in Vancouver it was the Lions and not the Kiwanis. Their enthusiasm was equal; indeed in Vancouver in 1953, they had us still working at midnight, with school choirs and bands still performing. We told the Lions that that was cruelty both to children and to adjudicators, and no way to achieve good performances from anybody!

Also in Vancouver I again met my old examiner Lloyd Powell, who had been living there for some time; and also an old fellow student from the R.C.M., the cellist Audrey Piggott, who was playing with the CBC Vancouver Orchestra. I also got to know the conductor John Avison, and the composer Robert Turner who, at the time, was working as a programme engineer. Some 12 years later he came to join my Faculty at the University of Manitoba.

At the smaller Festivals they made do with two of us, but the big ones needed all four; altogether we covered a great deal of Canada. That year we visited, besides Halifax and Saint John, Ottawa, Toronto, Chatham, Stratford, Winnipeg, Regina, Saskatoon, Calgary, Edmonton, Vernon and Vancouver. In fact, I pretty well followed the trail of the old English Light Opera Company of 1931-32. Only Fort William got no visit this time; it was not until 1966 that I did the Festival there, and by that time it was called Thunder Bay.

Four years later, in 1957, I came again to do the Canadian tour and visited the same places, except that in the Okanagan it was Kelowna and not Vernon. In Vernon I had met again Wilma Stevenson, with whom, at the R.C.M., I'd played in the original version of Arthur Bliss's *Two Piano Concerto*, with the composer conducting. It was nice to see her again. It is quite astonishing how many individual players one can remember years later, and with how many one meets up again in the musical profession. Over the period of two visits, four years apart, a number of those I heard have become well-known musicians; at least one of whom joined my Faculty at the University of Manitoba (William Aide), another ended as Dean of the Faculty of Music at Ottawa University (Cynthia Millman-Floyd), and another, Leon Cole, became a much-loved CBC host. Another Ottawa musician I first heard in 1953, Ishbel MacDonald, who was a beautiful pianist, became my wife in 1959. And I had the additional pleasure of getting to know a great many older Canadian musicians all over the country. What appears problematical, after so many years, is whether we actually did any good. I like to think we did, and I still do meet people who say they remember something valuable I told them 40 years ago!

After the 1953 tour I came back to England refreshed, and anxious to get back to my BBC work. The following year I visited Haifa for the ISCM Festival, and Paris for Alphons Silbermann's *Contemporary Week*. In Haifa I heard and met the LaSalle Quartet from Cincinnati, whose work I found so good that, over ten years later I brought them to Winnipeg to play Penderecki. In Paris I saw and heard John Cage for the first time; I was amused, incredulous, and finally shocked by the 'prepared pianos': I was not prepared! I still find it lunatic and unacceptable to spoil a fine instrument like a grand piano by sticking pins and erasers and other foreign bodies amongst the strings. And, I still find the resultant sounds idiotic and meaningless.

1956 took me to Warsaw; and 1957 back to Canada. This time it was not the Third Programme I was leaving behind, but the Home Service; altogether a less stressful affair. The Home Service existed for the 'middle-of-the-road' listener; nothing too abstruse or too long. Even though full of tunes, the Schubert *C major Symphony* was thought to be "too much for the Home Service audience". We had included it in a series of 'presented programmes' with an invited live audience and a Master of Ceremonies. This was Robert Irwin, a baritone who had had great vocal trouble, but who was eminently employable in this other capacity. He was (I'm sorry to have to say 'was') an Irishman of extreme cultivation and measureless charm. Irwin plus Schubert proved a very saleable commodity; no complaints about boredom or excessive length! Robert was my companion on the new Canadian Festival tour, which was just as engrossing as its predecessor. Even more so, because on this trip I made Ishbel's acquaintance properly.

In fact, Ishbel had played to me on my first visit to the Ottawa Festival in 1953. She was one of four pianists there who had made a big enough impression on me to cause me to search for their names in the programmes, when I came back in 1957. Sure enough, there was the name of Ishbel MacDonald. She appeared again, and played; and her beauty as well as her playing kept me entranced throughout the week or so of the Festival. When I was invited by the Registered Music Teachers' Association to return to Ottawa at Easter and give a short series of lecture-workshops, I accepted with alacrity. In between the workshop sessions there was, for Ishbel and me, a wonderful period of mutual discovery. We soon decided that indeed we did belong together, and although we had to wait for two years, while my previous, sadly unsatisfactory marriage was dissolved, Ishbel and her mother came to London, and we were married in the summer of 1959. As I write this, we have been together for 37 years; Ishbel has been a deeply caring and helping partner through all of that time. And the twenty-six years of age difference between us was something to be learned about and dealt with, which we have managed pretty successfully. It was hard for Ishbel's father, Roderick MacDonald, to accept me, once he had realized that I wasn't a "MacIsaac"; but by degrees he grew accustomed to his daughter's marriage. By the time of his very early and unexpected death in 1961, he had become reconciled to us; and his new and much-loved baby granddaughter Margaret surely helped that process! With my mother-in-law there was a good relationship which lasted for many years. Our two daughters, Margaret and Debbie, provided Granny MacDonald with much joy (and she gave likewise to them), and she lived until her 94th year, leaving us only in 1992.

Ishbel and I were married in the Hampstead Unitarian Church on Haverstock Hill. Many of our mutual friends assisted us, including our two mothers (my father had died in 1953), and we went to live in Mortlake. The address was aromatic; "Woodbine Cottage, Rosemary Lane", but the smell of the nearby brewery was stronger, and soon drove us away, to live in Pinner.

A year later, in 1960, I again had some Festival engagements in Canada, so we both went over; Ishbel to stay until the child she was carrying should be born. So Margaret came into the world in Ottawa.

My leave from the BBC would not extend long enough for me to wait for the birth, but a few weeks later I met Ishbel and Margaret together at Heathrow Airport, and we lived in Pinner for the next three years.

The English climate was not really good for Ishbel; she was never warm or comfortable in the winter until we had a good fall of snow. But I didn't realize just how unpleasant she must have found it until we arrived in Canada to live, and acquired a centrally-heated and air-conditioned apartment! I have since often wondered, with incomprehension, what degree of toughness the immigrants who settled the Prairies back in the last century must have needed. And their descendants, whether from the United Kingdom, Ukraine, Italy, the Orient, or wherever, are all now living in comfort and controlled temperatures!

Back to 1957, and Winnipeg. On this visit I had some serious discussion with Richard Cooke and his colleagues about the possibility of running a Music School in Winnipeg, and I told them that if anything should materialize, I would certainly consider coming out as an immigrant. Six years later this actually happened; and I found myself a resident of Winnipeg and, in due course, a Canadian citizen.

But I am anticipating events. In 1957 I was still installed at the BBC, making programmes, but without the zest with which I had tackled the Third Proramme. The new assignment seemed rather dull, although the excitement of the quarterly visit to Sir Malcolm was still present. Nor was I any longer obliged to listen to a lot of contemporary music. Instead, I found myself approached to help Lord Shrewsbury in his attempt to produce opera at his lovely home in Staffordshire, Ingestre. This proved an interesting and time-consuming occupation. It was not my usual line of country, and my ingenuity was tried quite a deal. I made the acquaintance of that excellent producer Anthony Besch; the conductor was John Pritchard, whom I already knew. Many of the members of the casts were known to me; and the operas we mounted were Bizet's *Dr. Miracle*; Purcell's *Dido and Aeneas*; Blow's *Venus and Adonis* (not properly speaking an opera); and Falla's *Master Pedro's Puppets*. There were also some concerts, of which the superb guitarist Segovia gave one. The only time I met him, though I'd often heard him in London and enormously enjoyed his beautiful playing. At that time guitarists were rare in England. I remember one enchanting evening in Wigmore Hall when he and Conchita Supervia gave a joint recital. Besides both being Spanish they were ideally matched as artists, and the result was magical.

In truth I was not sorry to leave the scene of contemporary music. I had been becoming more and more uncomfortable with it and its pretensions. For some long time I had been convinced (and nothing which has happened since then has taught me differently) that Schoenberg's wanton destruction of tonality as a viable means of writing music in the twentieth century, was a grave mistake. Dodecaphonic music seemed (and still seems) to me to be largely non-assessable by the human ear, since it was not allowed to provide any "sign-posts" in the way of key-points. It thus lost all anchorage and all possibility of contrast except by the less than accurate means of speed, pitch or dynamic. There can be no repose, because there is no way to relax tension by sinking back into your "home key"; there is no possibility of humour or real lightness (except in texture); the bare idea of a twelve tone operetta is laughable. Several sides of life are thus removed, and we are left with an undifferentiated species of aural squalor. I for one have always found this sort of noise arid and boring; and sometimes positively repugnant, the way it is with pornography of any kind. The composer seems to be thrown back on his own nasty, Freudian subconscious; in which I am not interested. Nor should I be; that is his affair, not mine. This desperately subjective stance I find off-putting, and sometimes definitely repulsive.

This is all crying over spilled milk, maybe; I know that one of the nastier (to me) efforts of Schoenberg himself, *Erwartung*, is now some 90 years old. But it is still unhealthy! Schoenberg (whom I have always thought was jealous of Richard Strauss; *Gurrelieder* is an unsuccessful attempt to out-Strauss Richard!) threw the baby out with the bath-water, and no one has been able to find it again. So we have all this wretched stuff by Webern and Nono and Stockhausen and Boulez. Pierre Schaeffer's *Symphonie pour un homme seul* (Musique Concrète) was amusing; but when he produced an 'opera' in Musique Concrète, using two singers, a loud-speaker, a harpsichord and a ladder, I thought he was being presumptuous. I bore with Stravinsky as long as I could (pace Nadia Boulanger!), but when he too, finally gave up and adopted the tone row, his blood had definitely turned to methylated spirits. The élan of his early works disappeared; instead we got endless *talk* about what he was doing, aided and abetted by that fellow Kraft, who got onto a good thing and milked it for all it was worth. And Igor *still* couldn't write a tune! The best "tunes" in *Petrouchka* will all be found to be folk-tunes; and the very memorable opening phrase of *Le Sacre* is only a couple of bars long. I do not find that everyone is tarred with this dreadful self-excavatory brush; it has been easy to listen to the few composers who have something positive to say, and are not eaten up with their own importance. Something other than subjective misery seems to inform the music of Britten and Lutoslawski; Dallapiccola did not have to make *Il Prigioniero's* condition even more disastrous by writing against the human voice; Penderecki can communicate the horror of Hiroshima without having to personalise it. *À bas les componistes-psychologistes: weg mit ihnen!!*

In my BBC years I indeed heard and arranged broadcasts of all kinds of music, from von Ficker's reconstruction of Perotin's *Sederunt Principes* (from around the year 1200 A.D.) to the latest Robert Simpson of the 1950s. So I cannot say I was unfamiliar with the commodity in which I dealt; I just cordially disliked a lot of it, and saw no reason whatever to jump on the *Tonreihe* bandwagon! I also suppose that, as the world has become increasingly noisy, brash and directionless over the past 75 years or so, I should not expect Art to be any different. I now have some sympathy with Bernard Shaw's Count O'Dowda in *Fanny's First Play*, though I used to consider him a rather precious ass. Or perhaps I am like the Elderly Gentleman in *Back to Methuselah* (Play #4) who "didn't approve of microscopes"!

One of the more interesting and remarkable figures of my time was Constant Lambert; composer, conductor, speaker (his performance of Walton's *Façade* with Dame Edith Sitwell was the best I ever heard) and writer on music. Lambert was a brilliant character in all aspects of his work, notably the musical-directorship of the Vic-Wells Ballet Company. But here, I want to remember him for his book *Music Ho!* which was written in 1933, and slightly revised fifteen years later. This book is a consideration of what has happened in European music, and therefore, by implication, in North American music too, since about 1900. He expresses a point of view with which I find it impossible to disagree, so nearly does it represent my own attitudes. Lambert was a most cultivated and intelligent man and his points are still valid, in my view. I would make *Music Ho!* compulsory reading in all English-speaking universities and music colleges. Lambert's only miscalculation was to overestimate the influence which Sibelius' music would have on subsequent generations. His assessment of the *Gebrauchsmusik* and *Tonreihe* schools seem to me to have been justified by events, as do his misgivings about Stravinsky. He explains (in the revised edition) his seeming neglect and underestimation of Bartok by pointing out that Bartok's really mature works had not yet been written when his book was being compiled. It was a waste and a tragedy that Lambert died so young (in 1951); though maybe, indeed, his work had been done. Now, 60 years after Lambert wrote his book, I still feel much the same as he felt then.

By 1958 I began to feel decidedly less at home in the BBC. In that year the beloved grandfather of all the musical profession in England, Vaughan Williams, died at the age of 86. The next year the BBC appointed William Glock as its new "Controller of Music". There was no connection between the two events; yet perhaps figuratively there may have been. Anyway, Glock proceeded to "control" in no uncertain manner, also taking over the job of Head of Music programmes, causing the departure of Maurice Johnstone; a pity for the BBC and a personal loss for me. Glock also brought with him, onto the staff, his friend the Viennese-born critic Hans Keller. Between them, these two "Schoenberg-ized" the BBC. No living composer who didn't write twelve-tone music could any longer expect to be taken seriously, or even sympathetically; and names like those of Edmund Rubbra, Bax, Ireland, Howells, Bliss, Jacob and others, gradually disappeared from the BBC's more publicized concerts and broadcasts. In fairness, it must be said that no attempt was made to denigrate the memory of Vaughan Williams, or to belittle Walton, Britten or Tippett. But tonal music was suspect; "out of date" was the phrase! Keller was the country's wildest Schoenberg fanatic, and he advertised his fanaticism with the typical modesty of the Viennese face to face with the "unmusikalische Engländer" (unmusical Englishmen). Two of his pronouncements irritated me so much that I have remembered them for over 30 years: "the only reason you can't whistle the tunes from a Schoenberg Quartet is that you don't know it well enough". (*Tunes?* In Schoenberg?). And "the Schoenberg *Violin*

Concerto (1936) is the first real violin concerto since Mendelssohn (1844)". This, of course, wipes out Brahms, Bruch, Tchaikovsky, Elgar, Sibelius, Prokofiev and Szymanowski, and even, believe it or not, Berg of 1935! When Antonio Brosa first broadcast the Schoenberg *Violin Concerto* in London, I found it ugly, unviolinistic, and cussed... but then, of course, I would!

This sort of heavily non-English over-emphasis may possibly have enlivened BBC programmes, but it did not enliven me! I spent a good deal of time trying to ensure that the "tonal English composers" continued to receive broadcast performances (in those programmes which I fathered) so that their performing rights incomes would not be too adversely affected. And I continued to place a Vaughan Williams work, large or small, in the programme for October 12th (his birthday), each year. In fact, V.W. ("Uncle Ralph") had become a musical hero for me. I admired all his music, and some I deeply loved. For the man, whom I had known since I was a student at the R.C.M., I had nothing but admiration bordering on reverence. And he would speak to *me*, a nobody, as though I were his equal. He appeared to me a very great musician, devoid of vanity, and his magnificent hymn tune *Sine Nomine* always reduces me to tears. It is for me the equivalent of Parry's *Jerusalem* and utterly beyond criticism.

I regarded the whole Viennese caper as a sort of "silly season" in rather poor taste; though it lasted quite a while because some members of the highbrow press encouraged it. The 'Old Guard' were definitely *out*. It caused me some wry amusement to remember that my non-doctrinaire friend Walter Goehr had been a Schoenberg pupil and had survived; and that my Hungarian friend Matyas Seiber also used tone rows but had retained his sense of humour, so had not become a Freudian mess. The BBC atmosphere became, for me, less and less congenial. I could feel myself being quietly edged into the corner to which Kenneth Wright had long been consigned; tolerance and courtesy, but no more influence. After almost 25 years, I began to feel useless.

Maybe Count O'Dowda was not so far different from me at this stage. The present affords me no sustenance, but in my time I have heard Casals play the cello and Rachmaninov the piano; Beethoven conducted by Klemperer or played by the Amadeus Quartet; Mozart played by Clifford

Curzon; Schumann by Myra Hess; Chopin by Cortot and Arthur Rubinstein. I have heard Elgar and Vaughan Williams under Boult; Walton under Sargent; Handel under Beecham; Huberman playing Tchaikovsky; Kubelik conducting Dvořák; both Oistrakh and Menuhin playing Bach, and Enesco conducting it; Brahms sung by Helen Henschel and Dietrich Fischer-Dieskau, and played by Edwin Fischer; Wagner under Bruno Walter; and Verdi under Toscanini. Can I now be satisfied with less? Where is the Bach to equal Casals? Certainly not Gould or Tureck. Where is the Debussy to equal Monteux? Certainly not Boulez or Karajan.

I think I have heard and known the best there was; and I am indeed fortunate. "For me the angels sing!" You can have the Tonreihen and Cage and Ives, and company!

So, when the University of Manitoba placed an advertisement for a Director for their new School of Music in the Daily Telegraph (I had been warned that it would be there!), I applied with alacrity. To my delight, and that of my wife Ishbel, I was appointed.[26]

1963: The Move to Winnipeg
The University of Manitoba

*I*N THE FALL OF 1963, Ishbel and I and our three-year old daughter Margaret arrived in Winnipeg. The "Three Musketeers" were still around and very lively. The University soon began a new building to house the School of Music and we settled down to a new and exciting life. Ishbel was glad to be back in her own country, and I was happy with new territory to work in. In 1965, the year of the School's official opening, the Amadeus Quartet came over and played for the occasion. Also in 1965, our second daughter, Deborah, was born; and so the Isaacs Quartet grew up in the middle of Canada. Here, my own love of music gained a new lease on life. Ten years later, in 1973, I became a Canadian citizen.

Our reception into Winnipeg life was made easy and pleasant by a variety of people, not least the "Three Musketeers" and their families. Sadly, at the time of writing this, none of the Three is still living. There was also the Reverend Donald Bruce MacDonald of Knox United Church, whom Ishbel (also a MacDonald) and her family had known in Ottawa. Donald Bruce and his wife Nancy were good friends to us for the time they both still lived. And there was Victor Feldbrill, then the conductor of the Winnipeg Symphony Orchestra, and his wife Zelda. I had already made their acquaintance when Victor conducted for the BBC in Manchester, and was really happy to see them again. In their home we first met that exceptionally fine man, the Chief Justice of Manitoba, Samuel Freedman, and his wife "Brownie". Freedman was also Chancellor of the University, and I attended the first Convocation after our arrival, and heard him give the Address. It was magnificent;

except for the content, I might have been listening to Mr. Churchill himself, or indeed, to the Prophet Elijah! I remember thinking that if affairs in Manitoba were run by such as he, the country was most fortunate. Mr. Justice Samuel Freedman is no more, and his equal in stature has yet to be found.

Then, in 1963 and for a while afterwards, there was the Directorate of the University itself, which was cultivated and enlightened in the persons who represented it; Dr. Hugh Saunderson, Dr. Harry Duckworth (a bit later) and Messrs. Waines, Chevrier and Condo. The School of Music got off to a very good start because of them. I ran the School for eleven years, until 1974, when the University rules decreed that I must retire, at age 65. Shades of Sir Adrian Boult being made to retire from the BBC at age 60; he was mad! I was too, rather. The School is still there, very much so; and so am I, twenty-two years later.

The translation from one office in the BBC to another office at the University of Manitoba was not too difficult to encompass. If equipped with enough telephones, an office is much the same anywhere (we had not yet arrived at computers and faxes). At the University, once the new School building was available, I had a big room with book shelves and a grand piano, and a gadget for silencing the phone-bell. I proceeded to try and build a school, buy pianos, arrange courses and teach some. I had little use for "desk musicians", other than composers, and decided that I would need to do my share of teaching as well as administering, and also would revive my piano playing. So, my office became a studio.

It was an interesting, and often an exciting time. Three members of my Faculty were already in the University's employ; two organists; the ever-courteous Ronald Gibson and the much younger and equally courteous Conrad Grimes; and the cellist Peggie Sampson. Peggie was much more than "just" a cellist. She was an excellent scholar, having been trained by two of Europe's most distinguished musical minds, Sir Donald Francis Tovey and Nadia Boulanger, and she had become a remarkably good and enthusiastic teacher of music in general. Her cello playing was also good; we played recitals together; and she had in some inexplicable way managed to survive Diran Alexanian in Paris. I met few other cellists who weathered him so well; his rigorous methods discouraged most of his pupils, and he did not succeed in producing another Casals.

Later additions to the faculty were people whose names became widely known across Canada: the pianists Alma Brock-Smith, William Aide and Harold Lugsdin; the composer Robert Turner; duo-pianists Garth Beckett and Boyd McDonald; singer Robert Irwin, whom I brought over from London; and organist Lawrence Ritchey, one of the finest Bach players I have ever encountered. I wanted my School to be a place where music was not only taught but also performed, and to a large extent I was able to effect this since I had faculty who were themselves performers. As the years went by, others were added: the harpsichordist and organist Douglas Bodle; the bassoonist and mediaevalist Christine Mather; the lutenist and scholar Richard Burleson; and a most accomplished and practical musician Ursula Rempel. I did not (and still don't) believe in a university musical department which is insulated from the community in which it exists, and so I made haste to establish good relations with the Symphony Orchestra (not very difficult, since Victor Feldbrill, the conductor, and I were on the friendliest terms); with the Winnipeg local of the Musicians' Association (AF of M) through their very intelligent and enterprising General Secretary, Joseph Karr; and with the Registered Music Teachers' Association, one of whose senior members, Jean Broadfoot, taught for the School. I do not think these close relationships have been maintained since I retired, and that is too bad. They are quite invaluable to an institution like the School of Music.

The results of these connections were soon apparent. One of the first chamber concerts given at the University after I arrived, contained the Schubert *Octet* (a novelty in Winnipeg in 1964) with the then WSO concertmaster Lea Foli, the conductor Victor Feldbrill as viola, Peggie Sampson, and other members of the WSO. Then, some little time later, we mounted the first Winnipeg performance of Schoenberg's *Pierrot Lunaire* with Sylvia McDonald (Boyd's wife at the time) as the singer, a group of musicians from the WSO and William Aide as pianist. The whole thing was made possible by a grant from the Music Performance Trust Fund of the Musicians' Association. Robert Irwin mounted a good student production of Purcell's *Dido and Aeneas,* and with the modest but valuable financial contribution of the University Administration we were able to arrange visits by distinguished musicians from elsewhere. I believed that this was a proper and necessary activity for a University School of Music; and by slow degrees the general public, as well as the University audience, began to attend our concerts.

During the first few years of the School's existence we had visits from the Amadeus String Quartet, the LaSalle Quartet from Cincinnati, the Chilingirian Quartet (Chilingirian was a nephew of my old friend, the violinist Manoug Parikian), the Alma Trio from San Francisco (a quite wonderful group); the pianists Abbey Simon from New York and Claude Savard from Montreal, and Alfons and Aloys Kontarsky from Berlin. Maureen Forrester came too, and contralto Helen Watts from London; and also from London came the violinists Alfredo Campoli and Erich Gruenberg, whom I have mentioned earlier as good friends as well as colleagues. With each of these violinists I collaborated as pianist and sonata-partner. Then there were student recitals, and Faculty recitals too. It was a very lively time, and one of which, as the years progressed, I became increasingly proud. It seemed as though what I had wanted to build for the University was right and worthwhile; and I know that it was being recognized in the rest of Canada. This I could sense from the attitudes of my colleagues from other universities, when we would meet at inter-university conferences and conventions.

Indeed, I made many good friends in other University Music Faculties; John Churchill, my colleague from the 1957 Festival tour, was at Carleton; Clifford von Kuster, whom I greatly liked, was at Western Ontario; Richard Eaton at the University of Alberta in Edmonton; Pierre Brochu at Laval; Helmut Blume of McGill; John Beckwith of Toronto; Graham George of Queen's; and Lorne Watson of Brandon. There were also Howard Leyton-Brown (an old Max Rostal pupil) in Regina, and Dave Kaplan, the clarinetist, at Saskatoon, where he succeeded Murray Adaskin. I still adjudicated for Music Festivals, both in English and in French; the latter for the Concours de Musique du Québec (afterwards "du Canada") run by Claude Deschamps. Through the CMQ I made acquaintance, and later a deep friendship, with that most lovable character Boris Roubakine. At that time, mid-1960's, Boris was teaching at the University of Calgary. It seemed that we had been fellow students at the École Normale in Paris in 1930; we had both been rather shy young men and had never met there! Boris and I were both glad to have repaired this omission, some thirty years later.

Many other names are associated in my mind with these festivals. I have already mentioned Gladys Whitehead, Martin Boundy and Charles Peaker; there were, too, Phyllis Schuldt (another Fryer pupil), Donald McKellar of Western Ontario; and later Robin Harrison in Saskatoon; and Dorothy Howard. My old pre-war friend Boyd Neel turned up in Toronto, not as a conductor but as an administrator; and also another whom I'd first met in London, Alex Brott of Montreal. All in all, it did not take long to feel that in Canada I was among friends, and Ishbel was too. The University took up a great deal of my time. Looking back on those first seven or eight years, I realize that I allowed myself to be eaten up by the School, and hadn't enough time and energy left over for my family. Easy to realize later, but hard to deal with at the time. I think that Ishbel, who always acted as a wonderful hostess to all who came through Winnipeg, was aware of neglect. I don't know if my daughters were also thus aware; they were increasingly involved with school.

As the girls grew up a bit, Ishbel was able to take on more private piano students, and thus boost her own professional activity. The piano at 948 Queenston Bay was in use as much as any of the pianos at the School. It was a lovely, warm-sounding Steinway grand, which had belonged previously to Leonard Heaton[27]. It takes some time to build a private studio of pupils, but after a while Ishbel's ability was known throughout Winnipeg and she was much in demand as a teacher. She still is! Besides Ishbel's students, and a few of mine, both our daughters learned to play, to one degree or another. There was music happening at work and at home, almost all the time; a rich atmosphere, if hectic, and I suppose we were all four fairly busy.

At the University I had the very strong support of the Administration (the men, in fact, who had appointed me), and this support lasted as long as Hugh Saunderson was President and Chief Justice Freedman was Chancellor, and while William Waines and Harry Duckworth were Vice-Presidents of the University of Manitoba. But Dr. Saunderson reached the age of retirement before I did, money became scarcer (the Government of Manitoba being largely responsible), the new Administration seemed less interested in the arts, and my budget for concerts gradually disappeared. At that time the University's age of retirement was 65, and that moment would soon be arriving for me. By the time we reached 1974 I felt I was having to fight for the School's continued existence as the sort of place I believed in; and into the bargain found myself up against an administrator whose only interest seemed to be to save money, and who thought a Music School should be running a Marching Band. I had no use for music being made into a "ra-ra-boys" exercise on the model of some American universities, any more than I had sympathy with bookish scholarship which never came to performance. One of my colleagues from another university once said to me "the trouble with you, Leonard, is that you're too damned European!" Well, yes, maybe I am. But music is to be performed and heard, or it doesn't exist!

The students' graduations were always a source of great satisfaction to me. Our B.Mus. course was then only three years in length, but it was a demanding one, and as far as humanly possible I made every single student get up at least once on the concert platform. And of course, there were those whom one couldn't keep off it!

One development which brought considerable kudos to the School was a Mediaeval Consort organized by Christine Mather, which brought to performance music of a kind previously unknown in Western Canada. It proved a great success, artistically, and travelled far afield; even to Aldeburgh in England, where my acquaintance with both Benjamin Britten and Peter Pears helped to introduce it. As it grew in reputation, its leaders grew in ambition, and soon there was not money enough in the School's budget to sustain its spreading activities. This resulted in an unfortunate tug-of-war, and the demise of the Consort.

During so many years in the BBC I had of course had to deal with multiple personal relationships, not only amongst colleagues but also with members of the profession in general. As BBC staff one was at a rather unfair advantage; no one wished to curtail his chances of engagements by getting on the wrong side of any of us. Indeed, I had one quite close violinist friend who refused even to visit me in the office for fear it should be thought that he was coming to tout for a job. Not everyone was so hyper-sensitive! In the University, personal relationships could be just as touchy, though I can honestly say that in eleven years, only three ever caused me distress; and only one in particular. I was not very adept at using the "promotion ladder" for my Faculty. I had made one or two staff appointments on the basis of practical musical know-how without paying much attention to formal academic standing. But of course, this is what a university uses in assessing academic prowess. I came from a society where "degrees" in music were unrelated to per-forming ability; this accounted for my engaging Robert Irwin[28], and bringing him over from England. He had no university degree, true; but he was a fine and cultivated musician, and had been a most distinguished singer of oratorio, lieder, French, English and Irish art songs and folk-songs. In fact, he was a thorough and experienced professional musician. This was enough for me; a degree could have added nothing to his knowledge and ability. Alas, when I tried to secure him a full professor-ship, the lack of a degree meant something to the University, and I got nowhere in this endeavour. Robert came to the conclusion that I was deliberately hindering his promotion, and ceased to speak to me or to Ishbel. Since, at our marriage a few years earlier, Robert had "given the bride away" in absentia patris, and Vera had been her Matron of Honour, this rift caused us both much grief, which was not lessened when Robert died, quite prematurely, a year or two after my retirement.

Another associate from the School's earlier years needs special men-tion. This was Alma Brock-Smith's husband, always simply known as "Brock", who became a very close and dear friend. Both Ishbel and I respected and admired him unreservedly, and I used to see him often when he was President of the Winnipeg Symphony Orchestra and I was a member of its Board. Victor Feldbrill had been winkled out of the Conductorship by the machinations of a small but influential group of Board Members (this caused my temporary withdrawal from the Board, since I felt I was being involved in something I regarded as profession-ally disreputable); the new conductor provided some very difficult per-sonal problems, and with these Brock-Smith coped in an urbane and civilized manner. His wife Alma (a very good piano teacher, by the way) had, hung on the wall of the hallway of their apartment, a photograph of Brock as a young man; it showed the handsomest and most dashing young man I think I had ever seen! Our first meeting, in fact, occurred in the elevator of the apartment block where we all lived[29]. We soon found out that Alma knew my old teacher Egon Petri, and that Brock mixed the most wonderful and potent "Black Russians", to which he introduced Ishbel, and later, me. Our then three-year old Margaret enjoyed their company too, though she didn't meet the Black Russians.

In the 1960's Winnipeg seemed to be a very civilized and quite sophisticated city. It is true there were certainly different strata of society, but great support was publicly given to all the arts; not only music. Ballet was a strong ingredient of Winnipeg culture, led by those two marvelously energetic and gifted women Gweneth Lloyd and Betty Farrally, whom we were fortunate enough to know. Choral singing was a Winnipeg enthusiasm, and was ably championed by the Men's Music Club, under the vital leadership of Dick Cooke (himself an expatriate Yorkshireman, brought up in the North of England choral tradition). The Philharmonic Choir and other smaller choral groups were, and still are, very much alive. Like the service clubs in other cities, the Men's Music Club of Winnipeg was indefatigable in its promotion of all sorts of musical endeavour[30].

Winnipeg had an Art Gallery, and in 1957 Ferdinand Eckhardt came from Vienna, to look after and expand it. Both of these things he did admirably, as well as becoming the Austrian Consul here for some years. He also brought with him his wife, Sophie-Carmen Eckhardt-Gramatté, known to their friends as Sonia. She was a composer of much energy and unbounded self-confidence, whose pretensions I was never, alas, able to take seriously. I thought she wrote inflated and derivative music, and I was impervious to Viennese musical "superiority". I was not taken in by what I found to be imitation Wagner, Mahler, Scriabin and Albeniz, and heavy Teutonic counterpoint. I had already had enough of this sort of thing in Europe! But, Sonia and Ferdinand could be both charming and generous, and good company, and they were very nice with our little Margaret. Debbie they hardly knew. Sonia died, accidentally and far too young, in Germany in 1974; her name has since been scattered around Manitoba, backed by suitably munificent gifts from her husband[31].

Much more sympathetic to me were the sensitivity and musicianship of people like Chester Duncan and Filmer Hubble. Duncan is a pianist and composer, though he has always earned his livelihood as a Professor of English at the University of Manitoba. The bulk of his compositions consists of songs, and the writing is spare, intelligent, and cleanly coloured. It is never pretentious. For some years, he and the school-master singer Orville Derraugh formed a partnership, and gave Winnipeg many beautifully polished performances of French songs and of Peter Warlock, of whose music I found Chester Duncan a most stylish interpreter. No one has followed Derraugh and Duncan, and today English and French songs are virtually unperformed in Winnipeg, except in the course of the annual competitive Music Festival.

Filmer Hubble was a church organist and choral conductor; a musician of impeccable taste, much ability, and warm humanity. For many years he ran a CBC broadcast series with a group known as "The Choristers". I found him and his family lovable people; in 1957 they looked after me when I came to Winnipeg to give a pair of lecture-recitals. Filmer was a musician of the type I admire so much; intelligent, informed, capable, sensitive, and a careful, punctilious teacher. I remember the performance of a young student of his, in a Winnipeg Festival, of the Mozart *D minor Piano Concerto,* which was beautifully prepared, trained, and wholly stylish. To my pleasure the student grew into a really good professional musician, and teaches at Brandon University, wherefore I saw him quite often over the years. His name; Lawrence Jones.

Chamber music has always been an "also ran" in the race for the public's attention, though in the last few years a group of players, headed by the concertmaster of the WSO, Gwen Hoebig and her husband, pianist David Moroz (once a student of mine), gives four concerts each season. The standard is extremely high and affords me, at least, great pleasure and satisfaction. But outside of this, the level of general knowledge, understanding and appreciation of chamber music is, for a city of Winnipeg's size, far too low.

≡XI≡

Retirement...?

*T*HE EARLIER YEARS of our life in Manitoba were perhaps the more musically vibrant ones; I have felt a gradual lessening of sophistication and of standards of taste. Or, it may just be my old age! Minimalism in music, the present idol, is to me, about as interesting as blind-man's buff; and as productive, too!

One aspect of Winnipeg's musical life which has been constant though, is the Symphony Orchestra. Victor Feldbrill brought it to a most excellent level, and into the bargain, used it to perform many works by Canadian composers. Regardless of their final worth, Victor felt that they should at least be heard, if only once. He gained the respect of all of us and the gratitude of the composers by so doing. We were sad when he and his wife Zelda and their two daughters left Winnipeg in 1968. He was followed here by George Cleve, Piero Gamba and Kazuhiro Koizumi; and then came Bramwell Tovey, from England, whose success has been phenomenal. He is the first since Feldbrill to be able really to identify with the community in which he lives and works, and his popularity seems to increase. He has even been able to introduce and maintain a week of contemporary music in this most conservative city. Its success is undoubted and quite surprising; and it brings the younger audience in, to stamp and whistle and shout. This is an astonishing development in this city of ours! It is certainly due to the magnetism of Tovey's personality more than to the inherent value of the music performed. But I cannot deny that this success, too, is a big asset in a place where the city fathers still look askance at an organization which doesn't make a big profit. I remember similar problems in Manchester; it took the Second World War to straighten that one out. But the WSO has always received enough support from the general public to keep going, and at present it is doing very well indeed. It has afforded Ishbel and me a great deal of pleasure, not only through its playing, but because we have made friends with so many of its members. Like all orchestras outside the very big centres, its string strength could be enhanced for some part of its repertoire, but it satisfies, and without it Winnipeg would be but a poor place to live. There is a second younger and smaller orchestra in town, the Manitoba Chamber Orchestra, but its impact is more subdued.

After my retirement in 1974 from being the Director of the University School of Music, my future seemed uncertain. And then my dear friend Boris Roubakine died, during an operation; and I was asked to take over some of his students at the University of Calgary until a new appointment could be made. I agreed to this, but before I could start, I myself had to undergo a gall bladder operation. So, in the late fall of 1974, I began a period of weekly commuting between Winnipeg and Calgary, which lasted for the rest of the academic year. It was a most helpful introduction to retirement, involving no administrative responsibility. I was able to enjoy it, as well as making new friends on Faculty, notably Willard Schultz and the Keaheys, Herman and Delores, who later turned up at the U of M.

I got back to playing the piano; not that I had ever really abandoned it. During the U of M years I had performed pretty regularly. Recitals with Campoli, Erich Gruenberg and Peggie Sampson have been mentioned; I also played a most enjoyable duet programme with Chester Duncan, and gave several solo recitals. My repertoire included Bach, the Brahms *F minor Sonata opus 5*, and a lot of Debussy, plus miscellaneous works by other composers. I believed (and still believe) that a Director ought to be able to show that he, too, is a working professional musician. I had excellent models before me: people like Mendelssohn, Bruch, Fauré, and Cortot, not to mention my own Director at R.C.M., Sir Hugh Allen, who was a gifted and inspiring (if rather frightening) choral conductor.

Once settled in at Calgary, I determined to bring to performance a work which I had always loved but never yet dared to play in public;

Schubert's great posthumous *Sonata in B flat*. It is a big undertaking, and I feel that it needs a person to play it who is wholly adult and experienced, to attempt to communicate its message. Schubert's very simplicity is deceptive and demands maturity, since it expresses such depth of feeling and such certainty, rather as does Mozart. Youth and enthusiasm is rarely enough[32]. The performances, first in Calgary and later in Winnipeg, gave me some satisfaction; I knew I had not been wrong to wait.

My formal connection with the University of Manitoba declined, naturally, and after a while virtually ceased. And my "official" life ceased too, after nearly 40 years in BBC and University. But I was not finished with the radio; the CBC had work for me, as a presenter of music programmes. My good friend Tom Taylor found plenty for me to do, over the next 7 or 8 years; studio programmes, public concerts, serialized talks, and special musical events like the CBC Festival, when many concerts were held in the St. Boniface Basilica. I became a sort of musical *metteur en scène* for the radio audience, and I enjoyed it all very much indeed. I wrote all my own presentation material; everything I had done up to now had prepared me for exactly such an occupation as this. Since that time, I think that "music presentation" has degenerated a lot. It is now largely required to be frankly didactic, or else semi-humorous, to neither of which attitudes would I have found myself sympathetic. Nor, I fancy, would the late Tom Taylor. I have little use for slightly condescending imparting of much relevant or irrelevant information at great length inside a programme supposed to be Performance, and I have even less time for desultory and inept humour in a miscellaneous music programme. I find it unsuitable and quite infuriating; it would certainly have made the men whose presentation at the BBC I had so greatly admired ill at ease, to hear what they could only regard as dreadfully amateurish work!

With the changing temper of society, music seems to have ceased to be an art, and has become a commodity, and I am now too old to play along! I see no generic difference between a professional and an amateur; either can be good; either can be efficient or inefficient; and either can be self-inflated. I can see absolutely no virtue whatsoever in "little Johnnie who can't read a note of music and plays so beautifully by ear". To me he is simply an illiterate and inefficient playboy. I do not think this essential need for literacy has changed, only I sense, to my displeasure, that the word "musician" is losing caste. Nowadays it is apt to mean the popular type of "music maker" who may or may not be literate, but who certainly does not waste his or her time playing Bach or Debussy.

The distance between popular and serious, as instanced by, say, Johann Strauss Jr. and Johannes Brahms, who admired each other, has been astronomically enlarged, and nowadays it would be hard for one type to hold the other in esteem. It is quite fascinating, if sobering, to see how each generation repeats what happened in the past, and grows too old to cope with the "Now" thing. A.P. Herbert, who wrote the book for *Tantivy Towers* (which my friend of many years ago, Maurice Hardy, played in) was quite right in his verse:

"As my old father used to say, in 1883...

And what was good enough for him is good enough for *me!*"

We watched our two daughters through school, with varying degrees of pleasure but always with some real satisfaction. We saw them becoming worthwhile human beings. The elder girl, Margaret, has become a professional musician too; a clarinetist and a CBC radio host. She seemed to find outlets for her performing ability and enthusiasms through school life and through some engaging and very friendly school music teachers. Debbie, five years her junior, had different needs, although she too took no small part in school music, almost despite herself! Her real love, however, was for sport, in one form or another. She tried almost every one of them, and left her enthusiasm for "straight" music behind. But the enthusiasm itself is what counts; it would have been so disappointing for Ishbel and me, if either girl had turned out apathetic and a dullard. This aside, Debbie had one school experience which caused us all some considerable frustration. This was her introduction to something called "The New Math", and she met it at the age of 7 or so. It consisted in having the teacher try to inculcate a sense of numbers without symbols or recognized procedures. It was a lamentable failure and was discontinued. But alas, Debbie had had to undergo its impact; she and her peers ended up unable to add, subtract, multiply or divide without the use of a calculator. I thought this was educational idiocy; rather of the same kind which, in music, offers short-cut routes to ability. There are *no short cuts*! Nothing, but nothing, is a substitute for the ability to work through one's own brain. Fortunately, this misguided mathematical behaviour on the part of the Manitoba Education System left no bad effects behind it, except purely localised ones; and in Debbie's case, she put these right at college. (In fact, now, she works often with quite convoluted maths, in her professional occupation as a federal civil servant).

I have grown deeply to distrust this kind of educational nonsense, supposedly designed to save trouble. It just doesn't, in maths or anything else. But where education means training for a job rather than training to be able to use the mind, no matter on what specific subject, this kind of short-cut must look very attractive. The proof of the indigestibility of this particular pudding was to be found in almost any store; the assistant could not give you change for a five-dollar bill, without working it out first on a calculator! Even a bill for, say, $1.50 caused too much cerebral disorder to do it in the head. This is humiliating. For someone of my age, brought up from "the year dot" on the multiplication tables, it seems little short of feeble-mindedness!

But, New Math apart, it was enthralling watching our girls through school, university, college, and into their work environments. It took a good deal of Ishbel's and my energy too! As the years have passed, the sort of job-training attitude in education seems to have intensified; and as I grow older I become more and more dubious about a system of public education which does not appear any longer to have as its goal the production of cultivated and informed individuals able to speak articulately and grammatically in English about subjects other than just hockey and computers. And I think, too, that this accounts for the general debasement of public taste in matters of Art and Entertainment. It seems to have been forgotten that Art needs an aristocracy of some kind (not merely financial, but mental aristocrats too) to support and nourish it. Once it was the Church, then it was the aristocrats. Who is it now? A terrible word has been invented to describe those whose entertainment includes classical music or good painting or serious drama or intelligent books, or any reading material beyond sports reviews, financial reports or crime; they call us "élitist". This is affording me no pleasure at all; I hate seeing a culture decimated by coarse mediocrity.

In more than thirty years' residence in this one Canadian city, Ishbel and I have made many good friends; perhaps none dearer to us than the Cooke dynasty; Richard and Constance Cooke's two daughters Audrey Belyea and Phyllis Thomson, and their husbands. All of them are in music, church, school, and concert. Audrey is a pianist and organist, and her husband Herbert a teacher of singing, a choral director, and one-time school maths teacher (not, I hasten to add, of the "New Math"!). Phyllis is an excellent soprano, and her Stewart, although an architect by profession, is an accomplished pianist, organist and choir director. His Anglican Church is one of only two in Winnipeg which still uses boys' and mens' voices in its choir. Our children and the Belyea and Thomson children, although rather different in age, grew up alongside one another, and the families have remained close, for which Ishbel and I have been (and still are) deeply grateful. People in whose company one can always feel comfortable and welcome; in other words, very good, long-standing friends, are a necessity in life. We feel very lucky to have friends like these; and there are more than I could possibly mention in one book[33].

We have also, of course, got to know many other places in this huge country. My work as a Festival adjudicator, as well as a university teacher, gave us the opportunity for quite a lot of travel in the 1960s and 1970s. We became acquainted with all Canada's major cities (except St. John's, Newfoundland; an omission which we hope to repair someday); and also many smaller places such as Vernon and Kelowna in the Okanagan; Yorkton, Nipawin and Humboldt in Saskatchewan; Trois Rivières and Rimouski in Québec, besides Québec City itself. And then there was that lovely place Banff, where I was delighted to be asked to teach in two different summers. There have been, for us, very pleasant visits to festivals or workshops in Ontario too; Sarnia, Waterloo, London, as well as the "great metropolis" of Toronto. We have yet to make proper acquaintance with the North, though I have been as far as Dauphin and Flin-Flon.[34]

But the place which has possibly given us all the most joy, children as well as grown-ups, is a tiny resort some 80 miles north of Ottawa, in the Gatineau hills. On the shore of Blue Sea Lake is a collection of cottages called Orlo, and there for some years we had our own cottage, made of fragrant cedar logs. Ishbel had known Orlo well in her girlhood, and her mother still had a cottage there, about a quarter of a mile from ours. Also, Ishbel's cousin Margaret Macdonald's cottage was only a stone's throw down a hill from us. The children especially, moved freely back and forth between the three places. It is a most gentle and picturesque spot; the lake is beautiful (and when we first were there, unpolluted) and the peace deep and healing. We shopped a few miles away, in Messines; and if some more recondite things than just groceries were needed, we could go as far north as Maniwaki. In those days, a small train still plied between Ottawa and Maniwaki, skirting the edge of Blue Sea Lake; I think everyone waved at the conductor as it chugged past! But now, that has been discontinued. All traffic is by road; fast and noisy; Québec drivers being, on the whole, somewhat boisterous and unpredictable. Sadly, we sold our cottage some years ago; 1400 miles each way between it and Winnipeg became excessive for only a fairly short stay. But we have become friends and stay in touch with the people who bought it, Gerry and Roger Wilson. And they became very close with our beloved Cousin Marg. We could, until 1995 still visit Blue Sea Lake, by staying with "Cuz"; but in June 1996 she passed away, very unexpectedly. A great loss. Blue Sea Lake was lovely, but we shall all miss Cuz'n Marg far more than any lake on earth!

I think it is time to stop. Clearly, like so many old people, I am becoming cantankerous! It is perhaps unavoidable, but my disquietude at the present condition of the art and profession of Music cannot be allowed to cloud the enormous joy which music has given me all of my long life. I have been permitted to describe a kind of professional circle in the sixty-or-so years I have been working: free-lance, radio, University, radio, free-lance, with intervals for the Donkey Tour and the RAF. And I have had wonderful company, both personal and professional, along the journey's route. It is strange to realize that it has all been the same person, moving from one constellation into another.

All in all, I am deeply grateful. I have found *so* much beauty in music, which I sadly fear is being denied to, or withheld from, today's young folk. I am resigned to being an old fogey; merely remarking, en passant, that I should find it absolutely incredible if anyone told me he experienced the same joy and ecstasy from a piece of late Stravinsky or

John Cage or Henri Pousseur, that I have always had from the Schubert *Two Cello Quintet*. The older I grow, the more miraculous the beauty; and the deeper my sense of humility before the very great composers, who are the gods' real messengers on earth.

Notes

1. "Charlie Fox". Uncle Carl had been a pupil of Cossman (Liszt's cellist in Weimar) and of Davidov in St. Petersburg. He lived until 1951.
2. Adolf Brodsky (1851-1929), a pupil of Josef Helmesberger. He gave the world première of Tchaikovsky's *Violin Concerto* in Vienna in 1879, instead of Leopold Auer who found it "unplayable". Brodsky later became the concertmaster of the Hallé Orchestra and the Principal of the Royal Manchester College of Music. His String Quartet (Brodsky, Rawdon Briggs, Simon Speelman and Carl Fuchs) was a noted feature of Manchester musical life for many years.
3. Arthur Catterall, violinist; concertmaster of the Hallé Orchestra 1912-1925; and also of the BBC Orchestra from 1930. He also had a String Quartet.
4. Frank Merrick, pianist, and his first wife, Hope Squire. They introduced me to their six cats, to Marmite sandwiches, and to the music of Vaughan Williams. Merrick was a Conscientious Objector and suffered time in gaol, stupidly and unprofitably. I was very fond of them both.
5. The Lener Quartet came from Hungary. Their first visit to England was in 1924, when they played in Manchester for my father, and in Glasgow for Sir Hugh Roberton. The members of the quartet were: Jeno Lener, Josef Smilovits, Sandor Roth, and Imre Hartmann. The

first three were pupils of Hubay, and Hartmann of David Popper. They became our very good friends, and had a tremendous success in England over a fairly long period of time.

6. John Lewis Paton, always known simply as "JLP", was Highmaster of Manchester Grammar School from 1903 to 1924, having previously taught at Ley's School, Cambridge; and at Manchester University College School. When he retired from MGS the school numbered 1400 boys (double the number he inherited in 1903), and he did not wish to cease working. He went on a lecture tour of Canada, and while there accepted the position of President of the new Memorial University College at St. John's, Newfoundland. He held this position from 1925 to 1932. Paton returned to England after his retirement from Memorial College, but continued to teach school in Kent, and throughout the 1939-1945 War. He died in 1946. A.G. Gillingham, PhD. said of JLP; "As students 21 years ago, we *all* stood in most profound awe of him; his exuberant energy, his sincerity of character, his great learning and earnestness of purpose." And John B. Ashley, PhD.: "Mr. Paton was a great Christian gentleman." (I am indebted for the foregoing information to Dr. Melvin Baker, Archivist of Memorial University, St. John's, Newfoundland).

7. Archie Camden was England's most distinguished bassoonist of the time. He left the Hallé Orchestra upon the formation of the BBC Symphony Orchestra in 1930, to take the position of principal bassoon under Adrian Boult. He never really retired, and could be found playing in this and that smaller orchestra into his old age. He was universally respected in the profession, and lived into his 90s.

8. Harry Jordan went to Buenos Aires as a young man "in business" and stayed for the rest of his life. He married an Argentinian woman named Corina, and they had 5 children. Albert became an engineer in gas (Buenos Aires Gas Company), and one of his brothers, David, was in the British Navy. The only other names I remember are Julia and Eric; the fifth cousin's name is no longer in memory.

9. She went off to the States, to teach at Smith College in Massachusetts. I had no further contact with her.

10. Barkis was a character in Dickens's *David Copperfield*. It's too long since I read the book to remember just *why* he was willing, or what

he'd do with his willingness. As a name for our donkey, after two days we knew it was a misnomer!

11. Wigmore Hall was *the* number one recital hall in which to play. A concert there meant that one had "arrived". It was where all the greats played; and now we were there too! We played Beethoven *Sonatas, opus 5 Nos. 1 and 2;* with the Debussy and Kodaly *Sonatas* in between. The notices were good, on the whole, with quite positive words from Constant Lambert; and also from Ernest Newman (see Appendix item #9 for Newman's review).

12. Anthony Lewis later became Professor of Music at the Barber Institute in Birmingham before moving on to the R.A.M.

13. ITMA = *It's That Man Again!* An immensely popular programme starring Tommy Handley.

14. Principal violinist with the Amadeus String Quartet

15. For those too young to know, Oswald Mosley was the leader of the British fascists.

16. This quartet started while all four were students at the Royal Academy of Music. They were, for a long time, Myra Hess's "quartet of choice" when she wanted to play chamber music.

17. Aubrey Brain had once come to R.C.M. to help us in the *Eroica*. It was the Second Orchestra, and I sat next to the great man, and marvelled that every note in the famous *Trio* sounded, no splits or fluffs; everything perfect. It was thrilling!

18. This was something which Kenneth Wright had done for many years on the Continent. Wherever I went in subsequent years in Europe, the first question I was asked by my European colleagues was "and how is Kenneth Wright?". He must have been one of the best-loved radio men in all of Europe.

19. The NordWest Deutscher Rundfunk Orchestra had been formed largely as the result of two British officials in the Occupied Zone, Howard Hartog and Jack Bornoff, taking a positive interest.

20. International Society for Contemporary Music

21. Erich Gruenberg, one of two violinist brothers who came from Israel, and studied with Max Rostal. Erich was the soloist; his brother, Eli Goren, was more an orchestral and chamber music player. Erich was a most sensitive violinist, and a joy to play with. He was

not as powerful as Campoli, but a classicist whose Mozart and Beethoven were lovely indeed. *And* I enjoyed doing Debussy with him.

22. In those days, concerts all began with *God Save the King* (later, *the Queen*).

23. She had been Hamilton Harty's wife, and one of the finest English dramatic sopranos. She was, at this point, about 80 years old.

24. Québec ran their own Festivals, known as the Concours de Musique du Québec; later, when they spread out across the whole country, "du Canada". These were run by a man called Claude Deschamps, and from 1960 I worked for him too.

25. Incidentally, in Toronto I had met again my old friend Elie Spivak, who had been a Brodsky violin pupil in Manchester, and whom I'd known since he was a teenager. A dear, gentle and lovable man; he died, much too young, in 1960.

26. I was not the only quondam adjudicator who ended up at a Canadian University. One of my companions in 1957 had been that civilized and engaging organist from St. Martin-in-the-Fields, John Churchill. He settled at Carleton University in Ottawa, and we were colleagues until he retired and went back to England.

27. Leonard Heaton was one of Winnipeg's senior piano teachers. He had come from Leicestershire, England in 1909, having been a pupil of Leopold Godowsky and Rudolph Ganz. We had met him on an earlier visit to Winnipeg, but he died a couple of weeks before our arrival in 1963. His widow was anxious to dispose of his two pianos and so we bought one (the Steinway) for ourselves, and the other (Mason & Hamlin) for the University.

28. Robert and his wife Vera were actually Dubliners, but were living in London.

29. Ishbel and Margaret and I lived there for only two years; then moving to a house in River Heights, which we called simply "948".... for obvious reasons.

30. It was also responsible for presenting a fine two-manual organ to the School of Music.

31. Ferdinand has died very recently, on Christmas Day, 1995. The Eckhardt-Grammatté Foundation will continue its work of promot-

ing the two great missions of Ferdinand's life: his wife's music and the art of Walter Grammatté, Sonia's first husband. Ferdinand is buried beside his wife and Walter Grammatté, in a grave in Germany which is now a historic site.

32. Mozart and Schubert may never have lived to be "old" men; but their music has the depth, wisdom and simplicity that normal humans only attain (if they attain it at all) with age and maturity.

33. Not only space, but also privacy, is a consideration here. We cherish all our friends, with thanks and with love.

34. Editor's footnote: Dad and Mom did in fact make it north to Alaska in August of 1997, on a one-week cruise, along with Audrey and Herb Belyea. Alaska was a place Dad had long wanted to visit, and though it was a short visit, his feet finally trod the ground at Skagway!

Appendix

1. Mr. Leonard Isaacs

There would be a great deal of sympathetic curiosity and serious interest in the public performance yesterday of Mr. Leonard Isaacs, gold medallist of the Associated Board local examinations and son of Mr. Edward Isaacs, the well-known Manchester pianist. The slow movement from Schumann's later *Sonata in G minor*, which Mr. Isaacs played, is not music which one would naturally choose to show off the executive powers or that one would think a fair test for the interpretive powers of a young player. But we think it turned out a very good piece to display the musicianly powers of young Mr. Isaacs. It demands in an unusual degree both penetration and a deliberate expressive power. It was in the last possession that Mr. Isaacs proved himself a musician so much beyond his years, and one, moreover, who seems likely to be far more than a mere player. The penetrating and severely sustained melody was given out with a quiet depth of feeling rarely found even in a mature player. When the accompaniment figures began to move with that full and living harmony which was so large a part of Schumann's secret Mr. Isaacs battled as capably and as little ostentatiously with the abnormal difficulties for a boy's hand. That Mr. Isaacs has ambitions as a composer also, and has already work to show which justifies them, is something which Manchester music-lovers will also regard with satisfaction, and not only for the boy's own sake.

Samuel Langford, Manchester Guardian, May 13, 1925

2. Civic Week and a Military Tattoo

To the Editor of the Manchester Guardian.

Sir: As a member of the younger generation of pacifists, may I add my protest against the inclusion of a military tattoo in the arrangements for Civic Week? It is an absurd assumption that a soldier is any less military in peace-time than in war. He is more so if anything; and half the good effects of the post-war peace work and League of Nations propaganda are spoiled by the continual parading of our "small but efficient" army before the country in such a glorified manner.

Pacifist says that we were never a military or aggressive nation. I should like to question that statement. He also says he likes to see the young manhood of England at healthy exercise: then let him visit a Boy Scout or Rover clubroom, or a local football field, where boys and men are not turned into fighting machines with no individuality and nevertheless get all the exercise they want. In the Boy Scouts one gets all the efficiency without effacing individuality, and without the bad effects of thinking always in terms of killing other men.

Why is it that we younger generation, who have grown up among the ghastly results of the war, and of militarism in general, and are striving with all our might towards peace and goodwill between us and our friends abroad, see on all sides, our army (unnecessarily large at present) advertised and flaunted before us in every possible way? Why have we, who are longing to show the world that it is possible to live on good terms with our neighbours; why have we to pretend to admire the army, which is the symbol of the militarism we so detest?

People are fond of saying that England leads the way nowadays. Then let it lead the new way, the only right way, and stop advertising militarism, as we do everywhere, in spite of belonging to the League of Nations. If a military tattoo is not an advertisement for militarism, may I ask what it is?

Yours, &c., Leonard Isaacs

Manchester Guardian, September 13, 1926

(just to show that Dad's frequent letters to the Free Press had an early antecedent.-ed.)

3. New Music by British Composers

Properly carrying out the function of a Municipal Orchestra, the orchestra yesterday (Friday) evening devoted part of a programme of British music to first productions of new works. It is definitely the province of a rate-aided orchestra to give young musicians a chance.

One of the works performed last night was a tone poem called *Punchinello* by John Greenwood, who, we understand, is a resident of Brighton. Of its kind, it is an admirable work, and, with ordinary luck, might well gain a place in the repertoire of British orchestras. It opens half grotesquely, half plaintively. Then it leaps along with laughing rhythms, with generous melody - here a little squeal of the pipes, there a little flutter of the drums. There is a hint of the showman, and a full quality of the accomplished musician.

The orchestration, for a full complement of instruments, is thoroughly sound, and the idea is carried through with individuality and consistency. Mr. Greenwood well deserved the ovation that greeted him at the end of the performance.

The other work performed for the first time was a *Concerto for Pianoforte and Strings* by Gordon Jacob. This is something of a very different order. It is advanced; advanced to the point of being revolutionary. The ear finds it difficult to get into sympathy with some of those many dissonances, and, frankly, if one had not known the orchestra so well, one might have imagined that the violins got persistently out of tune. The composer evidently believes in sharp contrasts and daring adventures into atonality.

The piece opens with a most promising rhythmic movement, with effective repetition. The composer also uses the device of repetition to good purpose in the second movement, where passages of the most forbidding character combat with moments of poetic charm. Mr. Gordon Jacob clearly has ideas, and intends to break away from conventions.

The extremely difficult pianoforte part was played with astonishing brilliancy by a young pianist, Leonard Isaacs. One was bound to admire the flexible sureness of his fingers and the memory that could carry him unfalteringly through such a whirling labyrinth of notes.

Brighton Herald, November 9, 1929

4. English Light Opera Company Stranded Here: Unable to Proceed to Ottawa for Opening Date of Next Engagement

Twenty-four members of the English Light Opera company, which closed an engagement in *Sinbad* Saturday night, are stranded in the city, unable to proceed to Ottawa for an engagement on Wednesday.

Working valiantly to keep going since November 28 when their Montreal backer gave them their last pay, the company today faced deportation as the only means of returning to the Old Country.

Members of the company are surprisingly cheerful in spite of trying experiences in their first trans-Canada tour. The company arrived in Canada in September.

From their opening in Montreal on September 21 to November 28 in Vancouver, members said that their performances of *The Beggar's Opera* and *Merrie England* earned money across the Dominion. When the second week's engagement in Vancouver showed falling receipts, their backer threw up his hands and left them stranded, Henry Jaxon, director of the company, said today.

Determined to make some effort to retrieve themselves, the company ransacked many avenues of revenue. Finally they decided to put on an English pantomime. During the six days before Christmas they worked feverishly at scenery, costume, music and rehearsals for *Sinbad* which opened on schedule on Christmas Day in Vancouver.

One girl member of the troupe designed 100 costumes and worked night and day with others in sewing them, rehearsing at the same time. Mr. Jaxon himself, scoured Vancouver for the music.

Although the Vancouver engagement was a success, the debts incurred left little money over. After playing Calgary, Edmonton and Winnipeg, the company found itself almost at the end of the rope. Because no bond was placed by their backer upon the entry of the company into Canada from England, deportation is apparently the only means of getting the company back to the Old Country.

C.E.F. Smith, acting divisional commissioner of immigration here, said today that he had not been officially advised of any action. It is understood, however, that the company has been in correspondence with the immigration officials at Montreal.

Members of the troupe had only the kindest words to say for George

F. Skinner, manager of the St. Charles hotel, where they are staying. They also revealed the fact that C.P. Walker had offered the Walker theatre and equipment free for a performance through which they might raise funds.
Winnipeg Free Press, February, 1932

5. Stranded Actors Are Given Help To Put On Show: Members of Opera Company in Happy Mood Despite Troubles

Low in funds but not in spirits, 13 actors belonging to the stranded English Light Opera company gathered on the steps of Grace church to be photographed by the Free Press photographer this morning. Henry Jaxon, director of the company, stated Mayor R.H. Webb had called a meeting at the St. Charles (hotel) at 12:30 for the purpose of organizing measures of relief for the company. Heads of various organizations and service clubs in the city who had offered assistance had been invited to attend. Final arrangements, Mr. Jaxon said, had been made for two performances to be given in the Walker theatre Saturday afternoon and evening. C.P. Walker is donating the use of his theatre; the musicians and other employees are also giving their services free.

The group was in a jovial mood as it gathered for the picture. The clothing of the men ranged from plus fours and llama coats to leather jackets. Dorothy Crofts insisted on removing her overshoes before the picture was taken because, she smilingly explained, she thought they were "revolting". There was a brief discussion by one or two as to whether they should get blankets to wrap themselves in.

"Hurry up," sang out one of the ladies, "because we've been promised real bacon and eggs after this." "Now then, everybody look hungry - I mean happy," jested another.

Promises of aid to the company have been received from the Princess Pat's band, the Musicians and Stage Hands union and the following Winnipeg clubs; Blackstone, Canukeena, Canadian, Cosmopolitan, Gyro, Kinsmen, Kiwanis, Lions, Rotary, Usadians and the Board of Trade. A Mr. Hewitson of Fort William Tuesday night wired Mr. Jaxon $100. Frank Shea led Winnipeg subscriptions with a substantial gift.

The performances the company will give Saturday will be in the nature of vaudeville.
Winnipeg Free Press, February, 1932

6. Westward Ho! With Music: Leonard Isaacs Off on Road Tour

Leonard Isaacs, the young piano pupil of Cortot, hailing from Manchester, and his cellist companion, Maurice Hardy, of the Royal College of Music, who are hiking Westward with a piano on a barrow to play on the roadside because they cannot get musical work, started on their great adventure bright and early this morning.

Long before London offices were opened for the day the two strolling players set off from Holborn. A friendly lorry driver gave them a good lift on their way by carrying them and their brightly painted outfit as far as Abingdon, the picturesque little Thames-side town near Oxford.

Their outfit was a thoroughly complete affair for music, and for a fairly comfortable rural existence even down to pots and pans. The only thing the adventurers had forgotten was the most important thing of all; a hat to collect the money. Having elected to make their wandering bare-headed they did not have a hat between them. By offering the loan of my hat and volunteering to lend a hand in pulling the barrow (ed. - the journalist invented this part, but it reads well!) I was permitted to accompany the adventurous pair on the first stage of their long trek, which will bring them somewhere in the neighbourhood of Weston-super-Mare in the summer.

Mr. Isaacs and his chum were in high spirits as the lorry bumped and rattled its way along the great West Road. Rain, the only thing they feared, obligingly kept off during the morning, and when the lorry dumped us all on the roadside about a mile from the town, the two players were keen to try the mettle of their itinerant music on the rustic community.

Lewis Hawes, Manchester Evening Chronicle, May 3, 1932

7. Rival to Modestine

Every listener knows Edward Isaacs. The Manchester pianist has given many microphone recitals. He has also invented a writing device to help out his own failing sight. Recently, through the medium of these columns, he offered to share this device with any blind listeners who might be interested. He received many hundreds of replies. Few listeners yet know Edward's pianist son Leonard, who broadcast from Manchester a fortnight ago. This summer Leonard Isaacs and Maurice

Hardy, the cellist, loaded a piano on a donkey-cart and travelled through the Western counties playing in their streets. They played popular stuff, but no jazz. Local girls' schools occasionally invited them in to give sonata recitals. Head mistresses were hospitable, let the vagabonds camp in the grounds, offered them the bathroom (while the girls were at breakfast). The donkey was called Mélisande. A friendly landlord, mistaking them for tramps, stood them a meal. Later he bought the piano, which reposes in a Somerset pub. Mélisande they sold in Dorset. She appeared none the worse for her four months of Brahms, Debussy and Chopin. A good adventure, this, recalling Robert Louis Stevenson and his donkey Modestine.

BBC Radio Times, October 7, 1932

8. She Ate Too Much

"Mélisande is dead," said serious-faced Leonard Isaacs to Maurice Hardy yesterday. They were in the artists' room at Houldsworth Hall waiting to broadcast in the Manchester Mid-day Concert.

"Oh," said Maurice Hardy. He paused from tinkering with his expensive cello and looked up thoughtfully. "How did she die?"

"Ate herself to death," replied Leonard Isaacs. He straightened his tie. "It was the death she would have wished."

"You bet it was," murmured Maurice Hardy. "You can just bet it was!"

Mélisande, happily, is not the name of an opera singer. Mélisande is the grey donkey made famous by Leonard Isaacs and Maurice Hardy six years ago, when, unemployed, no money, reluctant to sponge on their parents, they loaded an old piano onto a fruit barrow, took a tent and a cello, fastened the newly acquired Mélisande between the shafts, and went to seek their fortunes.

They toured England through all her more glorious counties, happily penniless, sleeping in strange places and earning money by wayside concerts from Beethoven to Herman Finck.

Word of them went ahead, and their reputation grew. They arrived in some little towns to find the concert hall ready booked for them. London recitals followed, and their names were made. With them, step by step on their pilgrimage to success, went Mélisande, the most sly, stubborn, greedy... yet sometimes strangely wistful donkey... you could imagine.

Now Mélisande is dead. News filtered up to Leonard Isaacs recently from the southern farm where he had left her. She had been sold to somebody else, who had unwisely omitted to put the barley-corn in a safe-deposit box. Mélisande ate the lot; about two and a half cwt.! And so, for two of Manchester's most promising musicians passes away the last link with their great adventure.

Manchester Guardian, sometime in 1938

(ed. - this date for Mélisande's death does not match Dad's recollection; but it shows how long the publicity and her memory lasted.)

9. Chamber Music

On Tuesday evening, at the Wigmore Hall, two young players, Mr. Leonard Isaacs and Mr. Maurice Hardy, took us through an interesting and unhackneyed programme of works for piano and cello. Though the cellist's tone was occasionally a little dry, the pair are so intelligent, and their performances so obviously directed rather to expounding the composer than to flaunting themselves, that it was a pleasure to hear them in whatever kind of music they undertook. It was good to hear again the neglected *cello sonata* of Debussy, that contains so much that shows the composer exploring new territory in his latest years, and the fascinating *sonata, opus 4*, of Kodaly, which, for all its seeming waywardness, is admirably controlled. Messrs. Isaacs and Hardy dealt as competently with these diverse modern styles as with that of the early Beethoven of *opus 5*.

Ernest Newman, The Sunday Times, April 9, 1933

10. Leonard Isaacs

F.R.C.M., A.R.C.M., B. Mus. (London). Musician. Born, January 3, 1909, Manchester, England; died of pneumonia following a stroke in Winnipeg, December 6, 1997, aged 88.

The word "musician" seems scarcely adequate to encompass Leonard Isaacs' many activities or the things for which he stood. Yet preeminently his world was the world of music, and in that world he played many parts. His obituary in the Winnipeg Free Press records that over a long career he was a "Festival adjudicator, examiner, composer, arranger, writer, conductor, lecturer, pianist, french horn player, teacher, accompanist, coach, mentor, freelance presenter and performer for the CBC." Yet this seemingly exhaustive list omits a number of specific roles of consequence, and does not speak of his interests beyond music.

Leonard Isaacs was born in England into a largely assimilated Anglo-Jewish family. His father had studied piano with Busoni and Leonard, having matriculated from the Manchester Grammar School, entered the Royal College of Music in 1925. There he studied with a number of eminent teachers, including the conductor Sir Malcolm Sargent. Winning four gold medals at the College, he went on to Berlin and to Paris, where he studied piano with the legendary Alfred Cortot. While in Paris he had the opportunity to hear another legend, Nadia Boulanger, give a talk on Brahms. The young Leonard passed up this opportunity, much later explaining sheepishly to his wife that he'd thought he already "knew" Brahms.

In the 1930s he toured Canada with the English Light Opera Company, gave recitals throughout England, orchestrated movie scores for the composer Richard Addinsell and conducted for Ivor Novello (at which time he also coached the actress Vivien Leigh in a rare singing role). In 1936 he began a long association with the BBC. Long before the CBC invented Radio 2, the BBC had its flagship Third Program, for whose music Leonard Isaacs had overall responsibility. From 1957 to 1963 he was in charge of general music programmes for the BBC. Through these years he worked with composers and performers like Sir William Walton, Ralph Vaughan Williams, Sir Adrian Boult, Sir Arthur Bliss, Benjamin Britten and Sir Peter Pears.

Several times in the 1950's he came to Canada as a festival adjudicator. In Winnipeg, adjudicator and city took to one another: in 1963 he was invited to become the founding Director of the University of Manitoba's School of Music, in which role he served for a decade. After retirement the pace, if anything, quickened: he continued to teach and lecture across the country, taught and coached privately, adjudicated in Winnipeg and elsewhere in Canada and the U.S. He wrote programme notes for the Winnipeg Chamber Music Society and for Symphony Nova Scotia. He wrote and broadcast for the CBC.

Leonard did not speak of musical "favourites," but he returned frequently to Debussy and inclined to the view that nobody since Bach had
done anything that Bach hadn't done first. He continued to perform
until the very end. Indeed, his final concert on November 2 (of Brahms'
F minor Piano Sonata) may have been the occasion of the first of several
small strokes leading to his final illness.

His leaving England, and his decision to become a Canadian citizen
in 1973, reflected an ongoing love affair with Canada that began with
his first visits in the 1930's. He felt challenged by the country's great
promise, by its capacity and willingness to take on new things. And he
became a passionate, patriotic citizen, whose ire could be roused when
he thought Canada was not meeting its potential. He was engaged with
the community and felt a stake in its direction and well-being. His letters to the newspapers - rather in the style of the late Eugene Forsey -
were pointed, elegant and feisty. Often about issues affecting the arts,
they could as easily be tart missives on Roseanne Skoke's homophobia
or the myopia of municipal politicians. He was, withal, a kind, gentle,
civilised soul, described by one who served with him through years of
committee work, as "a 'gent' in the oldest, truest, best sense of the term."

In Winnipeg, which takes pride in the range and quality of its cultural institutions, there were few such institutions that did not benefit from
his interest, support and assistance. He was a frequently seen and instantly recognizable figure at all sorts of musical events, from chamber music,
through Gershwin, to the New Music Festival. Through these and
through several generations of students and performers, his influence was
real and will endure. He was, if anyone merited the title, the Grand Old
Man of Winnipeg music.

He is survived by his wife Ishbel, two children by his first marriage,
Naomi (Munich), Nicholas (California) and two by his second, Margaret
(Halifax), and Debbie (Winnipeg).

*William Neville is a Winnipeg writer and a friend of the Isaacs family. From
the* Lives Lived *column of the Globe and Mail, January 8th, 1998*

Index